P8-CQK-192

# LONG RIFLE

# LONG RIFLE

One Man's Deadly Sniper Missions
in Iraq and Afghanistan

## Joe LeBleu

Former U.S. Army Ranger and Sniper Team Leader

The Lyons Press
Guilford, Connecticut
An imprint of The Globe Pequot Press

The Lyons Press is an imprint of The Globe Pequot Press.

All photographs © 2007, Joe LeBleu

Text design by Sheryl P. Kober

Maps @ Morris Book Publishing, LLC

Library of Congress Cataloging-in-Publication Data is available on file.

ISBN 978-1-59921-440-5

Printed in the United States of America

10 9 8 7 6 5 4 3 2

Author's Note: To ensure operational security for Special Operations commandos, faces of Rangers have been blurred. Also, other than the names of my fallen brothers in Afghanistan—Sergeant Bradley Crose, Corporal Marc Anderson, and Corporal Matthew Commons—no Rangers are named in this book.

THIS BOOK IS DEDICATED TO MY FALLEN BROTHERS IN OPERATION ANACONDA, AFGHANISTAN, MARCH 4, 2002: Sergeant Bradley Crose, Corporal Marc Anderson, Corporal Matthew Commons, 1st Battalion 75th Ranger Regiment, United States Army.

To Max Birchfield, whom I was fortunate to serve with and learn so much from in so little time—by far one of the best snipers ever. Though you have fallen, you'll never be forgotten.

For all those still in harm's way in Afghanistan and Iraq.

For my mother and father, who sacrificed so much, asking for nothing in return, and who were always supportive of my crazy ideas.

To my wife, Natalie, for your ongoing support through the years.

And to Mike Tucker, for making all this happen.

*Go tell the Spartans,*
*Passers by,*
*That here, obedient to their laws*
*We lie.*

—KING LEONIDAS

(Spartan commander at the Battle of Thermopylae, 401 BC)

*History teaches that when you become*
*indifferent and lose the will to fight,*
*someone who has the will to fight will take over.*

—COLONEL ART "BULL" SIMONS

(U.S. Army Special Forces, Raid Commander,

Son Tay Raid, North Vietnam, 1970)

*A CNN reporter asked a Marine sniper, "What do you*
*feel when you shoot a terrorist?"*
*The Marine just shrugged and replied, "Recoil."*

# CONTENTS

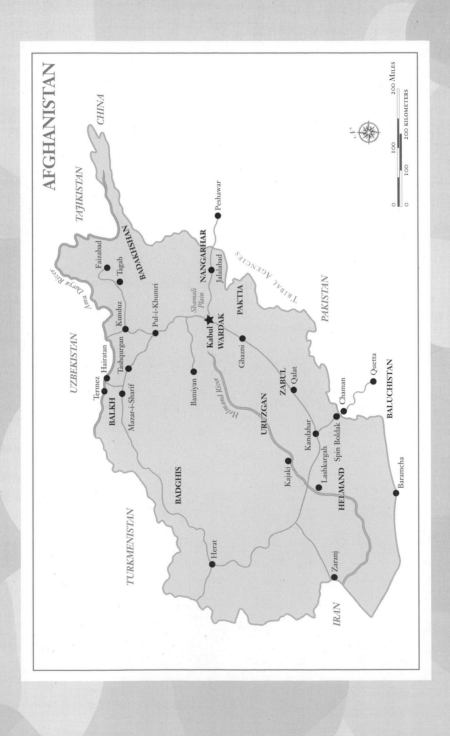

# AFGHANISTAN

CHINA

TAJIKISTAN

Amu Dar'ya River

Faizabad
BADAKHSHAN
Tagab
Kunduz
Pul-i-Khumri

Peshawar

NANGARHAR
Jalalabad

Shomali Plain

TRIBAL AGENCIES

PAKTIA

Kabul ★
WARDAK

Termez
Hairatan
Tashqurgan
UZBEKISTAN
BALKH
Mazar-i-Sharif

Bamiyan

Helmand River

Ghazni

URUZGAN

ZABUL
Qalat

Quetta

Chaman

PAKISTAN

BALUCHISTAN

Kandahar

BADGHIS

Kajaki

Spin Boldak
Lashkargah

HELMAND

Baramcha

TURKMENISTAN

Herat

Zaranj

IRAN

N

200 MILES

100
200 KILOMETERS

100

0
0

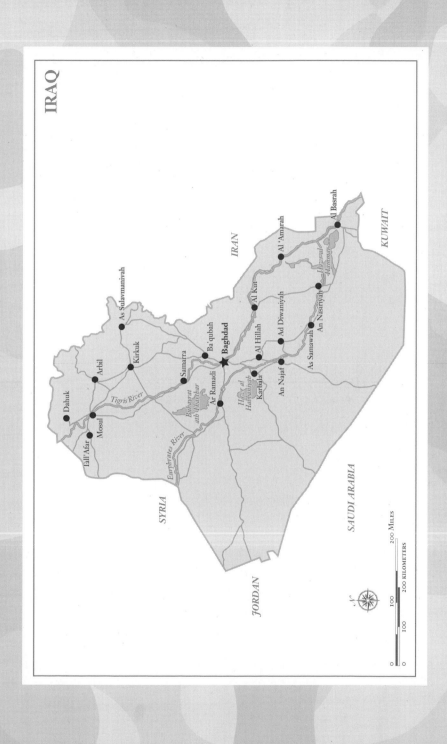

# Rogers's Rangers Standing Orders

Don't forget nothing.

Have your musket clean as a whistle, hatchet scoured, sixty rounds powder and ball, and be ready to march at a minute's warning.

When you're on the march, act the way you would if you were sneaking up on a deer. See the enemy first.

Tell the truth about what you see and what you do. There is an army depending on us for correct information. You can lie all you please when you tell other folks about the Rangers, but don't never lie to a Ranger or an officer.

Don't never take a chance you don't have to.

When we're on the march we march as single file, far enough apart so one shot can't go through two men.

If we strike swamps, or soft ground, we spread out abreast, so it's hard to track us.

When we march, we keep moving 'til dark, so as to give the enemy the least possible chance at us.

When we camp, half the party stays awake while the other half sleeps.

If we take prisoners, we keep 'em separate 'til we have had time to examine them, so they can't cook up a story between 'em.

Don't ever march home the same way. Take a different route so you won't be ambushed.

No matter whether we travel in big parties or little ones, each party has to keep a scout 20 yards ahead, 20 yards on each flank, and 20 yards in the rear, so the main body can't be surprised and wiped out.

Every night you'll be told where to meet if surrounded by a superior force.

Don't sit down to eat without posting sentries.

Don't sleep beyond dawn. Dawn's when the French and Indians attack.

Don't cross a river by a regular ford.

If somebody's trailing you, make a circle, come back onto your own tracks, and ambush the folks that aim to ambush you.

Don't stand up when the enemy's coming against you. Kneel down, lie down, hide behind a tree.

Let the enemy come 'til he's almost close enough to touch. Then, let him have it and jump out and finish him up with your hatchet.

—MAJOR ROBERT ROGERS (1759)

# INTRODUCTION

I AM EVERYWHERE AND NOWHERE. I EXIST TO NOT EXIST. I AM THE SHADOW my enemies fear. I am a well-tuned precision instrument that can change the direction of a war with one shot.

Most people know me as LeBleu (very few know me as Joe), and I've been called Snake Eyes a time or two, although I have little gift for shooting dice. But it's my time as a sniper at war in Iraq and Afghanistan, when I earned the nickname of Long Rifle, that best defines who I am.

I'm a former U.S. Army Ranger and sniper team leader. I grew up all over the world because my father was in the United States Air Force. My family has a long history of volunteering to go in harm's way, dating back to 1776. My great-uncle Ernie Simpson was a highly decorated Ranger in World War II and one of the first to join Darby's Rangers. He fought in North Africa, Italy, and throughout Western Europe. To this day all of his information is kept highly classified. He was one of the few Rangers to make it to the top of the cliffs on D-Day. He raided Mussolini's castle, just missing him by a few minutes. He was a prisoner of war more than a few times and somehow always managed to escape.

Ernie spoke of one time when he and a buddy were captured by a couple of Italian guards and thrown into a jeep. As they were driving down the trail, the guards discussed, in Italian, how they were going to kill the two men when they reached the end of the trail. Unfortunately for them, my great-uncle understood Italian. When they stopped, Ernie grabbed one of their knives, cut both of their throats, and drove off with their jeep. There was even a time when he was captured and lined up against a wall to be shot and yet somehow, he once again miraculously escaped.

His regiment started off with two hundred Rangers, and when he came home, there were just three left. He was the last Darby Ranger to pass away. Last I heard, his uniform and medals were given to a museum near his hometown in Oregon. This is a prime example of what it takes to survive war and retain the will to live, no matter what.

Six months after I was honorably discharged from the 1st Battalion 75th Ranger Regiment in March 2001, I was in lower Manhattan. I was there on September 11th when Al-Qaeda destroyed the twin towers of the World Trade Center—a day that changed my life and my country, forever. All Americans were New Yorkers on September 11th. For my generation, this was our Pearl Harbor.

This is my story of being at war in Iraq and Afghanistan.

One of the few things that kept me sane through all the combat I endured in Southwest Asia, and in the years since, was being blessed with my wife's love and support. On every desert reconnaissance in Western Iraq, through all the firefights in Fallujah, and in the mine-studded highlands and valleys of Afghanistan, she was always in the back of my mind.

I'd reunited with my old platoon on March 11, 2002, for the funerals of our fallen brothers, killed in action during Operation Anaconda in Afghanistan just a week earlier. I'll never forget those days for as long as I survive on this crazy earth. Each funeral started with a church service, followed by a graveside ceremony. We had planned to attend Anderson's and Crose's funerals because they were both to take place in Florida. Commons's funeral was being held at Arlington's cemetery, which very few of us could attend due to the fact that all the funerals were scheduled for approximately the same time frame. Besides, it wasn't really our place to tell the families when to bury their sons.

We attended Anderson's funeral first. I particularly remember standing outside as everybody else started to enter the small, intimate church. It never occurred to me how much strength I would need to gather, simply to walk into the church and see Anderson lying in an open casket in his dress uniform. I remember it seemed so surreal to see one of my brothers lying there, motionless—especially when it really didn't look like our Anderson. Because of his injuries, they'd had to partially reconstruct his nose.

Out of nowhere one of my fellow Rangers stood at attention and began reciting the Ranger Creed in a low but strong voice. One by one we moved together as a platoon once again, standing at attention, saying the Ranger Creed as one. Once we'd finished, nobody moved. You could have heard a pin drop. I think it was our way of taking a personal moment to say good-bye in our own way as we stood there as a platoon. We were all reminded again of why we'd chosen our profession. It was in our blood.

I was brought back to reality when we left the church. Reporters and photographers surrounded the church as if we'd just buried John Gotti. I'm not sure if it was because Anderson and Crose were some of the first Special Ops guys killed in action, or if they were just your regular antiwar, bloodsucking Liberals. Either way,

I was filled with so much anger and hatred—that this seemed to be the only thing the media cared about. God forbid the media show something with a positive outcome. Why? Because drama makes for better TV. I stopped and stared at them as if they were my enemy on the battlefield for what they were doing. I could barely maintain my professionalism.

The next day, we proceeded to Jacksonville, Florida, to put our Crose to rest in his hometown. Crose had to have a closed casket due to his injuries. One of the hardest things to sit through at a KIA (Killed in Action) church service is the roll call. The commander gets up in front and starts to call the names of the Rangers in that particular platoon. Each person called stands up at attention and replies "Here, sir." The commander continues down the list until he reaches the name of the deceased individual, such as Crose, and sounds off with his name—"Crose." A pause; no reply. He again sounds off with "Sergeant Bradley Crose." Again, a pause followed by no reply. Then a leader from the platoon sounds off with "Sergeant Crose is no longer with us. KIA." This is something you will never forget. The ceremony then continues.

Once the service at the church ended, we proceeded to the cemetery. As we drove away from the church we saw a few people on the side of the road, standing with their hats off respectfully, hands over their hearts. In the middle of my emotional war, I remember thinking, *That was odd.* Thinking it was nothing more than a few people who actually cared about the sacrifices that were being made on behalf of their freedom, we continued on down the street. As the car turned, we saw that both sides of the street were filled with red, white, and blue T-shirts, along with banners as far as the eye could see. We were stunned, and an eerie silence surrounded our whole convoy.

Everywhere we turned, everywhere we looked, the streets were filled with people holding banners that said things like "God Bless America" and "Thank you for your sacrifice." It ranged from a five-year-old kid standing in front of his school, to firefighters and policemen at parade rest, to an old veteran holding a stern salute as we passed. That day, literally, the whole city of Jacksonville was outside to show their respect for the sacrifice that had been made for them. As we sat in backseat of the car, in shock, I said to my long-term Ranger brother, Adrian Vizmanos, "I think Crose was more popular than we knew." We were both fighting back tears. Vizmanos was a short, stocky guy, full of heart, who would do anything you asked of him without hesitation. As we turned right onto the main strip that ran through the town, our windows were filled with patriotic people all the way to the cemetery.

As we walked up to the graveside, we all just stopped and looked at each other in shock, because like all Special Ops guys, we live in the shadows while everyone else reaps the recognition and benefits. We were used to this lifestyle and never sought recognition; after all, we'd chosen it. That's not why we did our jobs. It's a quiet profession very few will ever come to understand unless they've lived it.

We filed by and laid Ranger talismans on Crose's casket, such as Ranger tabs, Ranger coins, Unit scrolls, and other cherished items. The platoon was called to attention. "Present arms" was called, for us to give our final salute to Sergeant Bradley Crose, twenty-two, Orange Park, Florida; Corporal Marc Anderson, thirty, Brandon,

Florida; and Corporal Matthew Commons, twenty-one, Boulder City, Nevada.

Numb to our surroundings, we stared empty and endlessly as tears streamed down the faces of loved ones and our band of brothers, as "Taps" was played on the bugle and gunshots echoed throughout the cemetery. We held our salute for what felt like an eternity, until the sorrowful sound of "Taps" disappeared into the distance.

"Order arms" was called as we lowered our salute slowly and respectfully. Together, we recited the Ranger Creed as one to our fallen comrades. They had been killed by Al-Qaeda and members of the Taliban on March 4, 2002, while on a rescue mission for U.S. Navy SEAL Neil Roberts, age thirty-two, from Woodland, California, who had been captured and executed by Al-Qaeda. Rocket-propelled grenades (RPGs) had forced them to crash-land on the Takur Ghar mountaintop in eastern Afghanistan's Shah-I-Khat valley. It turned into a seventeen-hour uphill firefight in two feet of snow, which soon came to be known as the bloodiest battle of Operation Anaconda in Afghanistan, in March of 2002.

Word on the street was that the interpreter had sold us out to the Taliban, which wasn't uncommon. Terps (short for "interpreters") were known for selling Intel to the highest bidder. So the Taliban knew exactly who, what, when, where, and why. See, when it comes to the local Iraqis, whoever offers the highest dollar gets the Intel, which, in return, is transformed into a strategic ambush, because now they've had the time to carefully analyze and plan their attack. Basically, we were fucked from the word go.

I was always questioning what terps we allowed in the wire, asking, "Has anyone done any kind of background or affiliation check on any of these clowns?" You can take a wild guess on what the answer was. All I could do was just shake my head, knowing we were being set up for another ambush. Even the everyday Iraqi hired for work was scouting out the inside of our compound out of the corner of his eye while attempting to work. I would always say after our nightly mortar attack, "How ironic; the local Iraqis were just working here." Unfortunately the military is still learning from this mistake.

I'd served with Crose, Anderson, and Commons in Alpha Company, 1st Battalion 75th Ranger Regiment, Hunter Army Airfield, Savannah, Georgia. When Crose and Anderson joined the Rangers, I helped square them away. Crose was my roommate for a short while, and even though Commons came in just as I was leaving, he was still my brother, because once a Ranger, always a Ranger. Crose, Anderson, and Commons made the ultimate sacrifice for America without hesitation or ever asking why. They will never be forgotten. The Ranger Creed, recited by my old platoon at their funerals, binds us to all Rangers, of every generation. All Rangers memorize, live, and die by this creed on a daily basis.

## Ranger Creed

Recognizing that I volunteered as a Ranger, fully knowing the hazards of my chosen profession, I will always endeavor to uphold the prestige, honor, and high esprit de corps of my Ranger Regiment.

Acknowledging the fact that a Ranger is a more elite soldier who arrives at the cutting edge of battle by land, sea, or air, I accept the fact that as a Ranger my country expects me to move further, faster, and fight harder than any other soldier.

**N**ever shall I fail my comrades. I will always keep myself mentally alert, physically strong, and morally straight; I will shoulder more than my share of the task whatever it may be, 100 percent and then some.

**G**allantly will I show the world that I am a specially selected and well trained soldier. My courtesy to superior officers, neatness of dress, and care of equipment shall set the example for others to follow.

**E**nergetically will I meet the enemies of my country. I shall defeat them on the field of battle, for I am better trained and will fight with all my might. Surrender is not a Ranger word. I will never leave a fallen comrade to fall into the hands of the enemy, and under no circumstances will I ever embarrass my country.

**R**eadily will I display the intestinal fortitude required to fight on to the Ranger objective and complete the mission, though I be the lone survivor.

And what was true for my great-uncle and his brothers at Pointe du Hoc, Normandy, on D-Day, June 6, 1944, remains true for the Rangers of my generation, and every generation to come: *Rangers lead the way!*

Shortly after the burials of Crose and Anderson, we drove back to Savannah, Georgia. We were handing the military police our IDs to get back on base when the wife of one of the Rangers turned to me and said, "Hey, did you know today's your birthday?" Puzzled, I grabbed my ID, looked at it, and said, "Huh . . . how 'bout that? Happy birthday to me. I guess I forgot about it in all this fun."

We didn't say much as we drove on to the base, as we were mentally and physically exhausted from the funerals. Nevertheless, Vizmanos and I sat up all night laughing over old stories and trips we all used to take together while on leave. Thinking of the past with my fallen brothers, we talked very little of the funerals and the war going on.

Vizmanos and I knew what we needed to do, and by morning, we'd made our decision: We wouldn't stand on the sidelines anymore and do nothing while we watched all our brothers die.

I decided to return to active duty as a U.S. Army Ranger. I was in the exact same unit for six months, and then seized the opportunity to be a sniper. I knew we were at war and that I belonged with my brothers. I set out on a journey where I would soon be known as "Long Rifle," for my confirmed kill of an Iraqi insurgent at 1,100 meters in Fallujah during the autumn of 2003. To the best of my knowledge, that shot remains the farthest made in Iraq by any American or British sniper.

Ever since I'd entered the military, I had looked for a position where I could rely solely on myself and my rifle. I've always been fascinated by rifles and military tactics, and I've learned that I have a gift, an instinct that comes naturally to me in combat. For reasons known only to the Almighty, I have always found myself to be calmer and able to think more clearly under fire, and I've always known that I move faster and fight better when I'm on my own. It seemed like the crazier things got in combat, the more relaxed I became.

Coming of age in the Special Operations world as a Ranger, and working hand in hand with Delta Force commandos on highly complex and very sensitive missions, I had fulfilled my goal by kicking in doors and moving at 110 miles an hour on operations which remain classified to this day. There was no place in the world I'd rather have been. I felt fortunate to be among my brother Rangers and I was grateful for the incredible professionalism of the Delta Force commandos.

But somehow, I still felt like something was missing.

Though I'd come to understand the truth of one of Winston Churchill's maxims, after combat in the Khyber Pass in Afghanistan—"Nothing in life is more exhilarating as to be shot at without result"—I found that I still wanted to be in a position where I could penetrate deep behind enemy lines, relying purely on my own reconnaissance and skills. My gut told me that I'd really find a home as a sniper, and achieve what I'd set out to do.

Upon arriving at the U.S. Army Sniper School in Fort Benning, Georgia, on July 5, 2003, I really didn't know what to expect. I knew it was one of the army's hardest schools and it made Ranger school look like a vacation. I'd also heard many rumors on what a ball-breaker it was; for instance, folks had told me that the sniper instructors would smoke you until you couldn't move anymore. Indeed, I'd heard that some instructors smoked you until you couldn't even think. (*Smoke*, by the way, is U.S. Army slang for physical exhaustion.) There was even talk of having to hold your rucksack above your head until the sun came up, and being smoked until your sweat stained the concrete.

I entered Class 502-03 of U.S. Army Sniper School as Roster Number 11, or, as I was somewhat affectionately referred to by my instructors, "Snake Eyes." I soon discovered that all the rumors were true. I did stain the concrete with my sweat, as did every other sniper candidate. I never thought I could hold a sixty-pound rucksack above my head and still enjoy a beautiful sunrise in the beloved state of Georgia, but life is full of surprises.

Most sniper candidates are weeded out during the first week, due to very intense physical training, in addition to the physical fitness test with which all army schools begin. As with all physical training tests, you lose a handful of people right off the bat. Then we moved on to basic rifle qualification with the M24 7.62x51mm sniper rifle. In week one, you're assigned to a spotter; mine was Sergeant Flynt Warner, who would also be in my sniper section in Iraq. Warner later joined the U.S. Army Special Forces, where he continues to serve today on active duty.

Week one also consists of classroom and textbook curriculum from the *U.S. Army Sniper Training Field Manual* (the FM23-10), our bible, which includes instruction on ballistics, parts of the rifle, and scope mounting. Also, we had solid, hands-on training as far as zeroing your sniper rifle, knowing how to operate range and wind elevations on your scope, and making ghillie suits.

The ghillie suit, created by Scottish gamekeepers for hunting, disguises a sniper on virtually any terrain by breaking his outline and making him one with his surroundings. Ghillie suits were first employed in combat by British Lovat Scouts in World War I.

Throughout our training, we'd end each day in the "Ghillie Shack," where we performed rifle maintenance and constructed our ghillie suits, all the while talking shop about being a sniper.

Every night ended with each individual making a decision about whether they'd choose to have a little sleep, or no sleep at all. You could get a couple hours of sleep, and risk not being completely squared away for the next day's instruction; or, you could catnap, thereby ensuring that your ghillie suit, rifle, and gear would be 100 percent ready for the next day.

We started firing right away on the second day of school. Using iron sights on our sniper rifles, we fired at ranges of 200 yards all the way out to 700 yards. After our instructors—all accomplished snipers and U.S. Army sergeants, staff sergeants, and sergeants first class—were convinced we knew how to shoot with iron sights, we switched over to our Leupold 10x scopes.

Soon, the fat bodies had been weeded out; as with all elite U.S. military schools, U.S. Army Sniper School is designed to "force-drop" the weak candidates in the first week, and find out who really wants to be there. A key thing to understand is that the training is more focused on mental stress than physical stress, as the instructors want to see who will quit when things get tough. Someone who quits in training will certainly quit in combat, and could end up getting you killed.

We moved on to the nuts and bolts of sniping in the second week. Week two consisted of learning different types of firing positions, such as "prone supported"—lying on your belly with your legs spread to shoulder width, ankles flat on the ground with toes pointed out, with your sniper rifle supported by sandbags. In a combat situation, you would use anything nearby to support your sniper rifle, such as your rucksack, a window frame, bamboo, or a tree branch. All told, there are seven different firing positions taught to U.S. Army snipers: prone supported, prone unsupported, kneeling unsupported, kneeling sling supported, standing supported, standing unsupported, and the Hawkins (see glossary for full description of all seven firing positions).

The second week also covers vital lessons on reading wind, range estimation, and seeing trace—which means seeing your bullets trace to your target. At Sniper School, if you can't see trace, you will not graduate.

All instructors inform you from day one that in Sniper School, your spotter will make or break you: "Your buddy can fail you out of this school." A spotter is also a trained sniper who eyeballs targets for a sniper with a scope that is more powerful than the one on the sniper's rifle. It is up to the spotter to read wind, estimate range, and to follow the trace (or path) of the bullet to the target, so he can correct the shooter and help get him on target. Another crucial lesson taught in the second week is how to hold off, which many people refer to as *Kentucky windage*. This means knowing how to estimate wind and range with nothing but your naked eye and your gut instinct. Also, they taught us how to read *mirage*, which is the way the heat index mixed in with wind alters your vision of a target.

We were also taught how humidity and temperature affect the flight path of your bullet. A dramatic increase in temperature, for instance, such as a 20-degree increase, will raise the point of impact by one minute of angle (MOA). One minute of angle is equal to

1 inch for every 100 yards of range. So, if your target is 800 yards away, and the temperature is 90 degrees Fahrenheit, you're basically going to adjust about 8 inches lower on your shot. For instance, if you would normally aim at an enemy's center mass in normal weather, you'd adjust in tropical heat and aim at his stomach.

On the other hand, with a severe decrease in temperature, such as in arctic conditions, you'd raise your minute of angle by 1 inch for every 100 yards. So, in order to hit your enemy in the chest in snow-covered mountains, you'd aim at his head.

Humidity has basically the same effect on the bullet, but as long as you're adapting to temperature changes, you rarely have to adapt to humidity by itself. Generally speaking, adjusting for temperature is enough when snipers lock on a target in combat.

Last but not least in week two is learning the art of camouflaging. There are two types of camouflaging: natural and artificial. You learn how to adapt to your surroundings and how to make yourself disappear into bush, desert, jungle, and urban environments.

Throughout the rest of the course of instruction, we worked practically around the clock to master the art and craft of sniping, reconnaissance, and tracking. It was five weeks of intense, grueling, and very challenging training. Mornings regularly began at zero dark thirty, between 3:00 and 4:00 a.m., and we were lucky if we grabbed a couple of hours of sleep a night. Fifteen candidates dropped out from our original group of thirty-three.

Our hard work paid off in Iraq and Afghanistan. All of us who graduated had to achieve sniper marksmanship by hitting 70 percent of stationary metal targets at various unstated distances. Firing our M24s during sniper marksmanship, it was up to me and my spotter to figure out the wind and distance while being timed. We also had to pass range-estimation graded exercises, where we were given two minutes to estimate the range to each point using the naked eye, and the Leupold 10x fixed scope (M3A scope).

The target detection test was one of the more interesting; we had twenty minutes to draw a sketch of both panoramic and topographic targets. *Panoramic* is what you see in front of you; *topographic* is a bird's-eye view of a target. Our instructors also tested us on scanning targeted areas, such as rooftops, corners, windows, and doorways—anything out of the ordinary—with M22 binoculars and M144 spotting scopes. We also had to spot small objects, like antennas or a rifle sling, at a distance of 200 to 300 meters.

Before the penultimate Final Shot test, it was vital for us to pass a written exam that covered everything taught at the school, along with sniper history and a test of our stalking ability. Stalking is a sniper's bread and butter, and the most challenging part of being a sniper. We were even taught how to push a bush properly—softly and almost as if the wind had blown it—in order to maintain a covert presence.

While wearing a ghillie suit and carrying an M24 with three blank 7.62 rounds, we had three hours to move between 300 to 800 meters, set up in a firing position, fire two blank rounds, and identify a 6-inch letter on an 8-by-8-inch board, using only the twelve o'clock and six o'clock positions.

And then came the Final Shot test, where an instructor acted as our spotter and we shot two rounds at a target, exact distance unknown, between 600 and 1,000 meters. We had three minutes to engage the first target and two minutes for the second. We had to calculate our windage and elevation before firing. If you fail the Final Shot test, you're showing that you can't operate on your own, and you've failed the school; in order to pass, you'd have to start again on the first day of the next Sniper School—that is, if your unit allows you to re-cycle.

I passed my Final Shot test, and two days before graduation, I received my orders for Western Iraq. With the little time I had before I left, I returned back to the Scouts in 1st BN-505th PIR, and spent time with my wife and friends in Fayetteville, North Carolina. I began getting my gear mission-ready; I knew our combat tour would be at least 180 days, and could extend to a full year. Having received my orders in late August, I said my final good-byes to my wife, friends, and family, and by September 7, 2003, my brother Scouts and snipers and I were enjoying the pungent, fragrant aromas of Fallujah and Western Iraq—that enticing scent of buffalo manure, goat droppings, incense, diesel fumes, tire fires, raw sewage in the streets, and the body odor of Iraqi Arabs.

We were not the only 18th Airborne Corps unit in Fallujah. The U.S. Army Airborne Corps consists of three divisions: the 101st, the 82nd, and 10th Mountain. I soon found myself attached to Attack Company, 1st BN—32nd Regiment, 10th Mountain light infantry. It was good to be with 10th Mountain.

Exactly ten years earlier, my Ranger comrades at Mogadishu had been rescued by 10th Mountain light infantrymen on October 3, 1993. During a two-day action, two Delta Force snipers, Master Sergeant Gary Gordon and Sergeant First Class Randall Shughart, lived the Ranger Creed of never leaving a fallen comrade behind. Showing uncommon valor and extraordinary selflessness, they inserted from a Blackhawk into waves of oncoming mobs of armed Somalis, to save the life of a downed Blackhawk pilot, Chief Warrant Officer 4 Mike Durant.

Both Shughart and Gordon gave their lives to save Durant's life, and each received the Medal of Honor, posthumously. During my Ranger indoctrination period, I had met Staff Sergeant Mark Eversmann at 75th Ranger Regiment headquarters at Fort Benning. He had known Shughart and Gordon in Mogadishu, and had himself fought gallantly in the Battle of Mogadishu. In proving what a small world this is, former Marine and author Mike Tucker brought something to my attention in Fallujah on December 6, 2003: Two comrades of Shughart's and Gordon's from Task Force 1Ranger—1st Sergeant Nathan Fulks, Delta sniper at Mogadishu, and 1st Lieutenant Joe Thomas, a U.S. Army Ranger Specialist at Mogadishu—were in the same company in the 101st ten years later, in combat in Mosul in that autumn of 2003.

Fresh out of Sniper School and now at war in Iraq, I was the "go-to guy" for sniper missions, reconnaissance, and gathering field intelligence. I was the only former U.S. Army Ranger in the Scouts, and people didn't hesitate to attach me to missions right away, night and day. Little did I know that I was headed into seven months of dust, sweat, and bloodshed in Fallujah and Western Iraq, into some of the heaviest combat I have ever seen. We were in the heart of Iraqi insurgent and Al-Qaeda terrorist activity. At that time, U.S. Central Command (CENTCOM) had designated Fallujah as the most dangerous city in Iraq.

We had entered the eye of the hurricane.

## BOOK ONE:
# Dust, Sweat, and Blood

THE MINUTE I STEPPED OUT OF THE BIRD ONTO KUWAIT SAND, THE HEAT immediately started to choke me as if somebody was holding a hair dryer set on incredibly high heat right in my face. It was like being locked in an oven. I had arrived in early September 2003. Dust swirled all around me, caking my face and hands and boots with fine sand, the heat blanketing me like I was in a sauna with the dial spun all the way up.

I remember thinking, this should be interesting. This wasn't my first rodeo, but it *was* my first combat as a paratrooper sniper. I had just spent five weeks at Sniper School, training and maneuvering in jungle environments, and here I was, standing in the middle of the desert in the Near East, saying to myself, "This should be fun." I knew that I would be doing more than the other Scouts simply because I was a brand-new Sniper School graduate. It is common in any U.S. Army Scout platoon to lean heavily on the school-trained snipers. Additionally, everyone in command knew that I was a Ranger veteran.

Soon, we arrived in Western Iraq, dust drifting up off our boots as we walked off a C-130 at Al Taqaddum Air Force Base. Sand dunes rolled low and golden west of the tarmac and heat mirages glimmered on the runway like rivers as we carried our rifles, fighting knives, and war gear off that bird in the stifling Mesopotamian heat.

Gearing up for my first mission in Fallujah, September 2003, I checked over my gear and weapons, and made a few last-minute adjustments to my ghillie suit. I was somewhat chagrined to find that Task Force 1Panther was, to me, not really mission-ready. The lack of organization told me that I'd be walking in the dark for a while. By my analysis, the intelligence section did not exist at all at that time. This was more than troubling for snipers in particular, because it's imperative that we obtain fundamental details of an area and culture. It's standard operating procedure in combat to receive important basic information from the intelligence section, such as the average height of men in the country, along with things like standard window and door measurements.

In early September 2003, we got none of that. The absence of a Coalition unit in Fallujah for the six weeks prior to the arrival of the 82nd Airborne prevented Captain Love, an intelligence officer for Task Force 1Panther, from having any appropriate intelligence for the battalion as a whole, and especially for the Scouts. In no way was it the fault of Task Force 1Panther, nor the United States Army on the whole, that President Bush had no battle plan for Western Iraq, nor any understanding of how to fight and win a guerrilla war in the Near East.

A veteran clandestine agent from Near East Ops, Central Intelligence Agency, told Tucker in Manama, Bahrain, on September 4, 2004,

Bush had no plan for Western Iraq, and his essential plan for the entire war was, victory means securing Baghdad—there was never any question, in Bush's

White House, of "What happens if we get in a guerrilla war in Iraq, because we haven't committed to killing the Baathists?" Well, never assume. Outside of the Kurds, we have no allies in Iraq. And as you damn well know, Baghdad was never secured. We continue to take live rounds 24/7 in Baghdad, IEDs, RPGs, ambushes of all kinds, mortar rounds, and rocket attacks. That's not mission accomplished; that's mission goatfuck.

As a sniper in combat in Western Iraq in early September 2003, without any field intelligence to prepare my data, I knew that I'd have to rely purely on my training and my instincts. I realized that it would be up to me to gather my own field intelligence and bring my sniper team, especially my spotter, up to speed.

On September 7, 2003, in Fallujah, I was busy preparing myself and my spotter, Specialist Steve Eggleston from Los Angeles, California. Eggleston was young, a quiet, blond-haired paratrooper who was fit and tough, and on his second combat tour with the 1st-505th, having already served in Afghanistan for a year as a paratrooper. Iraq was his first combat tour as a sniper and Scout, and his natural inquisitiveness and physical stamina helped him a great deal. On that first day in Fallujah, I was schooling Eggleston and the Scouts on what to look for during upcoming missions when word came down for our first mission.

After my briefing in the mid-morning, I prepped my gear and weapons and my team did the same. As a sniper team leader, it's vital to ensure that your team and spotter are always mission-ready. I led a three-man sniper team, which was uncommon in the U.S.

Army sniper world. A sniper team usually consists of a shooter, plus a spotter/radioman, who is known as an "RTO" (radio transmission operator). For the Scouts of 1st-505th, however, we were in three-man teams. Private First Class Arroyo from Los Angeles completed my team, as my radioman. Two teams loaded up into the Humvee including mine. Eggleston carried a suppressed M4 (an M4 5.56 caliber assault rifle with a silencer), while Arroyo carried an M4/M203 assault rifle/grenade launcher. Arroyo was about the same height as Eggleston, a shade under six feet, and very lean, with dark eyes set back deep under his eyebrows, like a hawk, and short thick black hair. Clever and hard-core about being a Scout and sniper, Arroyo was quick-witted and sharp in the field. He learned quickly; I rarely had to tell him anything twice.

Operating in a desert environment in the Near East in that kind of heat can be difficult, but it is nearly overwhelming when you're carrying sixty-plus pounds of gear. Sweat dripped from our eyes and immediately began soaking our uniforms; the sauna-like heat was nearly choking on that late summer day in Western Iraq. The extreme temperatures, reaching 125 to 140 degrees Fahrenheit in Fallujah in early September 2003, made it challenging—especially when there was no way to escape it. Even our drinking water was hot, but that's all we had. There's nothing like having a nice canteen full of hot water.

Our first mission in Fallujah came down that morning. Our Scout platoon sergeant was Sergeant First Class Richard Lopez, a beefy, straightforward, career staff noncommissioned officer (NCO) and also a former Marine Scout/sniper. Lopez came into our hootch that morning, hands on hips, and said, "Load up and roll." His deep, gruff voice boomed as he nodded in the direction of our Scout Humvees laagered outside in the sand and gravel.

Lopez was a real no-nonsense guy. When he first came into the army in December 1990, not long after his honorable discharge from Marine infantry, he'd ordered a 101st trooper at Fort Campbell, Kentucky, to remove a gold earring. The soldier had cursed him and refused, so Lopez ripped out his earring, telling the bloodied trooper, "Only pirates and cheerleaders wear earrings. Last time I checked, you're a soldier in the 101st! No skull and crossbones do-rag on your head, and you're not wearing a cheerleader's skirt. No fuckin' earrings!" With the 101st, Lopez had carried a machine gun and fought in Iraq in the Persian Gulf War.

Arroyo and Eggleston were already in the back of the Humvee in the mid-morning heat before I got there, their Kevlar helmets and body armor on with full combat load, magazines jammed in vertical mag pouches over their body armor. Sweat poured down their faces. As we loaded up, I noticed that no one wanted to drive, so I volunteered. Staff Sergeant Jason Martin, twenty-seven, from Lynchburg, Virginia, rode shotgun. Martin was a cheerful, easygoing guy who could crack wise with the best of us. About six foot even, lean and broad-shouldered, on that day he carried an M4 assault rifle. Ranger/Airborne–qualified and an Afghan vet, he was also a school-qualified sniper and a sniper team leader.

I jumped in the driver's seat, did my checks—"Everybody ready, everybody in, tow strap up?"—and Sergeant Patrick McGuire, a shooter, shouted back to me, "We're good—let's roll."

Our Humvees were naked, in grunt parlance, meaning we had no armor beneath us, no armor on the sides, and plywood above our drivers' heads for a shooting platform. We didn't even have sandbags or doors. We were attached to Attack Company, 10th Mountain light infantry, the third vehicle in the convoy. The lead vehicle, carrying 10th Mountain, had a mounted .50 caliber machine gun. We rolled out from our hootch and linked up with their convoy, staged just inside the wire at the South Gate. It was burning hot. Everybody was good to go and once outside the gate, we began to roll.

We headed to the Cloverleaf, which was the intersection of the two major highways in Fallujah, Highways 1 and 10. No one had briefed us yet that the Cloverleaf was a known IED magnet, where many roadside bomb attacks and coordinated ambushes had gone off on Third Infantry Division soldiers in the summer of 2003. I soon learned the hard way that you should always blow through overpasses and intersections, rolling fast and furious in fear of IED ambushes. Going off my instincts that morning, I shouted out, "The Cloverleaf looks like a good ambush site. Look for wires, trigger-men—for anything out of place!" I was trying to get my team into the same combat mentality that I was in—more or less, on the same page with me. Unlike me, none of them had seen action before, and I wanted them to have that edge you need to survive in war.

At that time, no patrol from Task Force 1Panther had yet entered Fallujah. As we were entering the city, I was yelling back to our sniper teams, "Now, it's game time! This is real! Make sure you're pulling security! Make sure you're scanning every corner, alley, window, door, rooftop!" Fallujah's trash-strewn streets were filled with the scent of diesel, and always, the acrid smell of burning tires and raw sewage.

As I was driving and scanning for enemy, I was taking mental photographs of the city and remembering key landmarks, such as mosques, how the apartments and housing were set up, how staircases would lead up to the rooftops, and whether there were fire escapes on houses and buildings. I was also looking to see how many people were out on the street and what they were dressed like, what their daily activities were, watching eye movement and checking hands for pistols and knives, and observing how people were reacting to us being there. Always scoping hands and eyes, always looking ahead for alley corners and rooftops where enemy snipers would likely be.

Given that it was everybody's first mission in Fallujah, you could feel the tension all around you, like a cloud hanging over all of us. Even though there was nothing but sun that morning, that cloud was damn sure there. As I was scanning and collecting data, we came to the end of the first dusty, stinking street. I noticed a group of Iraqi men all wearing their red *khaffiyehs* ninja-style, wrapped completely around their heads and face, with only their eyes exposed.

As they all stared daggers at us, cold death stares, I remember saying out loud, "That was odd." I made a mental note about *red headdresses on groups of men*. Seconds after observing them, the convoy came to the end of the street and turned left. As my vehicle was turning left, our convoy suddenly disappeared into smoke. Dazed and confused, I had no idea what had just happened. I didn't realize I had just been through my first IED ambush. At first, all I heard was ringing. Then, I began to hear tires screeching and the squealing of brakes. The driver of the Humvee in front of me had slammed on his brakes, stopping right in the center of the kill zone.

I was convinced that my legs had been blown off since I had shards of concrete all over my lap. I glanced down and found that my legs were still there, although they throbbed and ached from being slammed by the concrete. The pain was intense. Like the rest of us, my TC, Martin, was groggy from the blast of the IED. There was a huge crater left behind from the blast, likely caused by at least three 155mm artillery rounds wrapped with detonation cord, and possibly, also wrapped with plastic explosives.

In any kind of convoy ambush, you never stop; you blow right through. But combat can unnerve anyone, and to be fair to that soldier behind the wheel in front of me, it was most definitely his first patrol in Fallujah. As I was getting my bearings on the Humvees in front of me, I was also doing a status check on my snipers. We started taking AK fire from all directions: rooftops, alleys, and streets. We were now in the middle of a coordinated ambush, set off by the blast of the IED. I remember AK fire raining down on us and yelling, "It's an ambush, it's an ambush!" I really feared for our snipers in the back of our Humvee, who had no mounted heavy weapon and no cover. Eggleston, Arroyo, Warner, and McGuire were basically sitting ducks, totally exposed to enemy fire from rooftops surrounding us and alleys in all directions.

I started shouting to the 10th Mountain soldiers in front of me, "Move, move, move!", none of us knowing if the driver in front of us was dead or alive as the vehicle just sat there. I pulled around the immobile Humvee with my snipers laying down heavy suppressive counterfire. As I wheeled around it, in the same motion I grabbed an M4 with my right hand. Throwing the rifle over my left arm for leverage, with my left hand on the wheel, I began returning fire while evasively driving us out of the kill zone. I kept returning fire to my left where we were getting hit hard, muzzle flashes flaming from an alley. I emptied a magazine rapidly, shooting single shots. Clearing the kill zone, I yelled back, "Changing mags!" McGuire laughed when he heard me shout that I was changing magazines, because it's something you should never hear your driver say in combat.

My magazines were doubled, which is slang for taping or joining two mags together, for fast reloading. Somehow, by the grace of God, I was able to hit the magazine release button on my M4 with my right hand while keeping my left hand on the wheel. I made sure the mags fell on my lap, and I grabbed them with my right hand and inserted the fresh magazines. Meanwhile, the bolt had locked to the rear, as with all M4s, so I turned my M4 sideways, pushed the rifle forward very hard so that the bolt release hit my forearm, and chambered a new round. I yelled, "I'm up!" to let my snipers know that I was reloaded. McGuire laughed again. I looked back now and could see Warner standing up, with the .50 caliber Barrett sniper rifle shouldered, scanning the windows and rooftops left to right, looking south—totally focused, but, nevertheless, an easy target for the enemy.

Now we were the second Humvee in the convoy. I remember yelling back, "Is that Humvee up yet?", trying to find out if the immobile Humvee was damaged and if there were any 10th Mountain guys killed in action. McGuire shouted, "Roger, it's rolling!"

Once the convoy was back as one, we moved up the road a mile and stopped, so that our Humvees were staggered on both sides of the road, with each Humvee covering the fields of fire of the nearest Humvee. This is known as a "herringbone" formation for mounted vehicles. We got the order immediately. "Dismount and pull security!" Cars were approaching from the kill zone.

I jumped out of the driver's seat and yelled, "Stop those cars! Hold the people and search them! Search the vehicles!" Meanwhile, 10th Mountain checked for casualties, and we all did our status reports: checking rounds, water, and any wounded or killed. Before we got back in our Humvee, I gathered my sniper team and said, "Welcome to Iraq, boys; that was one hell of a welcoming party." My team and McGuire grinned, shaking our heads, feeling it was somehow incredible that we were alive, all of us miraculously unwounded. You could feel the tension disappearing in the desert heat around us.

The best medicine to get someone's mind off of pain and fear in war, I have found, is comedy. Humor calms people down in combat—especially people who are wounded or who've just seen their first action. Seeing my sniper team and the snipers and Scouts with us now at ease after our first action in Fallujah was good, I remember thinking. I recalled many times as a Ranger when I'd joke with brother Rangers and Delta Force commandos after being under fire, and how the tension would fade and a sense of calm and clear focus would return to us. In my experience, when you are calm while in combat, you think more clearly and are able to move smoothly, while still maintaining speed, keeping the element of surprise.

The lead and second vehicles told us we had two 10th Mountain brothers wounded with shrapnel to the legs. We designated the first Humvee as our medevac vehicle, and put our two wounded on it. The medic told us, "We've got to get these guys exfilled, now!" due to loss of blood. We had no time to plan routes out of Fallujah, so we turned around and hauled ass. There was no medical station at Camp Volturno, located on the outskirts of Fallujah, so we pushed on to Forward Operating Base St. Mere, about three miles east of Volturno. It was a race against time to get our wounded brothers to the medics' station at St. Mere so they would survive.

Once they were stabilized at St. Mere, the convoy headed back to Volturno to refit, rearm, and regroup for night patrols. Before we headed out that night, we were told that due to my team's actions in the counter-ambush, we had killed twenty-two insurgents.

Back inside the wire at Volturno, I pulled Warner aside and asked, "What the hell were you doing with the Barrett? What if you had shot that thing from your shoulder, standing up? It would've blown you out of the vehicle!" I didn't mean to make fun of him— okay, I did—but at the same time, I also wanted to make damn sure that he wouldn't make that same mistake again. Both of us were laughing by now, and he said, "I don't know . . . That was just the first thing that came to my mind at the time. Ain't adrenaline a bitch!"

I slapped him on his shoulder good-naturedly and said, "I don't think I'd do that again; it might hurt." Smiling and laughing, he shrugged and nodded. "Yeah, I guess so." We walked on, happy to get back in the wire in one piece, all of our fingers and toes in place. We were damn grateful to be alive.

We headed out the wire on foot that night, on a reconnaissance patrol into the desert near Fallujah. For night patrols, I would switch scopes to the PVS-10, which is a day/night scope.

That night, I made sure that I carried the PVS-10, due to its versatility and reliability. Also, there's no need to "re-zero" the PVS-10; you can mount it on different sniper rifles quickly, with no loss of accuracy when it comes to putting rounds downrange. Once a set of slots on the rail system of a rifle is chosen, the same set of slots should always be used in order for the rifle and scope to retain its zero. I would always take a knife and mark where I wanted my scope to sit directly on the rail system. Even in complete darkness, on a moonless night, I could just feel where the etch was on my rifle and know exactly where to mount my scope.

Going over the wall that night, I carried my M24 sniper rifle and my 9mm Beretta sidearm, worn on my right thigh with one magazine in and two magazines on the black nylon Blackhawk drop holster. Our Scouts and snipers were all in a concrete hootch located thirty meters from the fifteen-foot-high wall, a wall that enclosed all of Volturno. It was easy for us to "jump the wall," as we put it, climbing up on ladders to cross over and jump down the other side. At the same time, I was always thinking to myself, "If it's this easy for me to jump the wall, then it's got to be easy for the enemy to jump the wall."

Sleeping so close to the wall, only a mile from downtown Fallujah, insurgents and terrorists could have easily jumped the wall and slit our throats. Keeping that thought in mind, we would sit outside our hootch at night in the shadows, staring at the wall, our weapons at the ready. I remember saying to McGuire, "I sure wish insurgents would jump this wall, so we could have some fun." McGuire, gregarious and jovial nearly all the time, would smile and say, "Hell, yeah!"

Paratroopers and 10th Mountain warriors guarded the base from four very distant guard towers, and other towers in between the main four were unmanned at times. So, we Scouts and snipers took it upon ourselves to guard that section of the wall near our hootch on Volturno.

That night, we moved slowly on the reconnaissance, the first of many night patrols to come. No matter how much we would do during the day, we knew that we'd always be going out at night, on foot, for reconnaissance and to gather field intelligence. My M24 felt heavy in my arms; it was thirteen pounds including scope and rounds, with a free-floating barrel and excellent balance, but I soon got comfortable with it on night reconnaissance. With the M24 I always had one round chambered and five in the magazine, with ten more rounds in a sleeve on the buttstock, and thirty more rounds in my rucksack. There's an old saying in regard to the M24: "If you shoot more than five rounds, you're having a bad day."

The night reconnaissance went without incident, and like nearly all the night reconnaissance we did in Fallujah in the fall of 2003, we got on the horn to our Scout radio watch as we headed back in, saying, "I'll call you back five minutes from now, at the wall." A Scout would wait for our second call, then toss the ladder over the wall. We'd set up a tight defensive perimeter, covering 360 degrees of security, back to back, with all points of the compass surveyed. Then, we'd peel off, one by one, swiftly going up the ladder and jumping down on the other side. The last man over would pull the ladder up and toss it down on base.

Night and day, throughout September, I was on more missions than any other sniper. Although I was sweat-soaked and tired and hungry all the time, I was always mission-ready. My grueling first tour in the army as a Ranger really prepared me mentally and physically to deal with the constant daylight combat and night reconnaissance missions. I remember telling my team, "Who gives a shit; we'll get all the sleep we need when we're dead, and I don't intend on dying just yet." I said that a lot throughout the tour in Fallujah, and my team would smile and Eggleston would say, "Roger that." They must have really thought I'd lost it; no doubt, my pearls of wisdom kept them on their toes. The unbearable heat was perhaps more tolerable to my men than my humor. Between the desert heat in Western Iraq and the constant, around-the-clock missions, I lost ten pounds during the month of September.

As a sniper attached to 10th Mountain, I was getting hit going out the wire, by IEDs and coordinated ambushes and RPGs, and getting hit coming back in the wire; it was 24/7 action. Upon reflection, it was understandable. After all, we were at war.

From a commander's perspective, it was wise to use my team for so many sniper and reconnaissance missions, given my background and the field intelligence I'd already gathered that September. I recall Mike Tucker saying to me in early February 2004, over coffee, "Outside of the Delta commandos here, you're the only warrior in Task Force 1Panther with *beaucoup* experience on missions with Delta Force." I just grinned as I replied, "Huh . . . I guess so. Here's to dodging more RPGs." But he was right.

As Major Kirk Windmueller of U.S. Army Special Forces has said, and it's a great philosophy on dealing with combat, "Things could always be worse, and I could've been dead a long time ago."

One night after coming in, following a period of three very intensive, grueling weeks of combat and reconnaissance, I was sitting on Eggleston's cot when 1st Lieutenant Swartwood walked in and told us that he was pulling us off missions for forty-eight hours, due to the fact that we'd been in more IED ambushes and seen more combat than the entire battalion. The lieutenant felt we were stressed to the breaking point. I later found out from Mike Tucker that Swartwood had written me up for a Bronze Star with "V" for Valor, for the September actions in Fallujah. The lieutenant, no doubt, had our health and welfare in mind and wanted us rested and ready for upcoming missions.

I was still very game to stay in the fight, around the clock. Somewhat chagrined, and realizing I could do nothing but look at it as a small joke on me, I had to laugh when I found out we were getting pulled off missions for forty-eight hours. I remember looking at Eggleston after the lieutenant told us to stand down for two days and saying, "Can you believe that? We're pulled off missions for forty-eight hours. We can't do anything. Maybe we should let him know there's a war going on."

My philosophy on war is that war is war; you have to keep driving on, learning to improvise, adapt, and overcome—and how to drive a stake through your enemy's heart. You win wars with guile, deception, and excellent human intelligence. Sun Tzu was right three thousand years ago when he said that spies are the key to victory, and he'll still be right three thousand years from now.

Relentlessness, ruthlessness, a fighting spirit, and total commitment to victory are required. Unity, strength and guile, sacrifice, commitment, and an unrelenting desire to kill your enemy and crush his will to fight are what wins wars.

Your leadership has to be willing to say, "Bleed with me," and *live* it, not say, "Go shopping with me, and fill up your gas tanks, and let somebody else bleed. The nation that stands together, fights together, bleeds together, suffers together, struggles together, and sacrifices together is the nation that wins together." If your leadership does not call for total commitment and total sacrifice, you will lose.

When you've got a president and commander in chief like Franklin Delano Roosevelt in WWII, you're in good hands. FDR understood that demanding sacrifice from the American people is essential to victory in war. Like Churchill, FDR totally understood that winning wars means calling on people to give their blood, sweat, tears, and toil. And FDR also understood that victory at war comes from killing your enemy, not from trying to pay off your enemy, as Bush has discovered in the Iraq War. Money is not ammunition. And when you make the mistake of confusing money for ammunition, that will likely be the last mistake you'll ever make at war.

No one ever won a war by shoveling piles of money at the enemy —and the Iraq War is stone-cold proof of that in our time. It goes way too far off into left field to come back for a smooth transition.

I made sure that my spotter and team enjoyed the downtime for two days. I took it upon myself to make sure that the intelligence section, headed by Captain Love and Captain Zawachesky, had all of my field intelligence so they could disseminate it to the battalion and companies, to ensure that our paratroopers and 10th Mountain boys would not walk into the same black hole that I'd walked into. I walked down to each company in Task Force 1Panther on Volturno: Alpha, Bravo, and Charlie companies of the 82nd Airborne, and Attack Company, 1st Battalion 32nd Light Infantry Regiment of 10th Mountain Division. I wanted to confirm that Task Force 1Panther S-2 was correctly disseminating the intelligence that I was giving them, down to the companies. Unfortunately, S-2 was not disseminating all of the field intelligence I'd gathered, although some of it was getting through.

My intelligence on red *khaffiyehs*—which I'd highlighted in my field intelligence to S-2 as "The Curse of the Red Ninjas"—did get through, thank God, and it was good hearing from paratroopers and 10th Mountain grunts that they understood. "When we see the red ninjas, we know they are enemy and possibly triggermen for IEDs."

Once I felt like everyone had been given the heads-up on what to look for and be aware of, I spent my last twenty-four hours of the two days off giving classes to our Scouts and snipers on target detection, range estimation, and different ways of scanning for enemy in Fallujah. Basically, anything I could do to keep my men on a keen knife edge, to keep a combat mentality, I did. In my last twenty-four hours of stand-down, I also cleaned my rifle and sidearm, checked my gear, counted rounds, and logged in information

35

and field intelligence in my "dope book," which is basically a logged record of all shots fired from that sniper rifle, as well as intelligence gathered in the field. I made little side notes of key things to remember and look for, such as the average height of men in the area, the typical size of car windows and car doors, the size of doors on houses and apartments, and other information vital to striking at insurgents and terrorists in Fallujah.

I'd also made sure that all of my team's weapons were always clean and ready for the next mission. A clean rifle will never fail you, but a dirty rifle will get you killed. It is crucial that a sniper team leader really sets the example not only for the Scouts and snipers on his team, but also for the entire platoon.

I've found that the hardest thing to accomplish in the open desert is for you and your rifle to blend in, so I would carry my sand-painted, desert-camouflaged M24 sniper rifle by one extended bipod leg, hanging down by my left leg. I did this because it's the best way, in an open desert environment such as Western Iraq, to hide not only the sniper rifle but also the scope from the enemy's sight. I also held it that way so I could easily bring it up to fire. My backup weapon was a standard military issue sidearm, a Beretta 9mm semiautomatic, carried on my upper right thigh. I always had one magazine jacked in and two on the side. Each magazine held fifteen hollow-point rounds, staggered. I was still somewhat skeptical about relying on a sidearm up against AK-47s, but this sidearm was all the backup weapon I had.

Therefore, I always carried a minimum of five knives on me. One was on my left shoulder, taped to my vest. That was my "knuckle knife," for extreme close-quarter battle. The grip on a knuckle knife enables you to maintain your hold in hand-to-hand combat, and it is a very effective close-quarter edged weapon. I also had two mini double-edged commando knives—a 2-inch fixed-blade version of the Fairburn-Sykes British commando knife of WWII—laterally looped to the back of my belt, on my lower back. My fourth knife was a 4-inch blade, double-edged, fixed-blade boot knife, located on the inside of my left leg with the sheath taped to the top of my boot with military-issue 100-mile-an-hour tape. And number five was a Smith & Wesson Bullseye extreme ops knife attached to the inside of my right boot. My uncle had carried a similar throwing knife as a U.S. Army Special Forces commando in Vietnam.

I taped all my knives to my body with 100-mile-an-hour tape. That way, if I had to run, I knew the sheaths would stay in place; also taping the sheaths was necessary to maintain noise discipline, which is essential to survival at war because the smallest, seemingly insignificant things, like a rattling sheathe, can give your position away and get you killed. To some people, this may seem excessive, but as the American infantry proverb states, "Your knife will never run out of ammunition, nor jam on you."

The reason for my boot knives being taped to the inside of my legs, rather than the outside, was for one, if you get into hand-to-hand combat, it's harder for your enemy to locate and grab your knife and use it against you. Also, by having it on the inside of your leg, it's hidden, and if for some reason you're knocked to your knees, you can grab your knife quickly and thrust as you spring up, without the enemy knowing. It's very difficult in actual hand-to-hand combat to see what someone has in their hand as you are standing above them, with all the adrenaline pumping through your veins.

One thing that Delta Force commandos taught me thoroughly was the absolute necessity for understanding both the philosophy of effective hand-to-hand combat and additionally, superior methods for both hand-to-hand unarmed combat and close-quarter battle with knives. The Delta Force philosophy on hand-to-hand combat is very wise and practical, rooted in common sense: Kill your enemy in three seconds or less. You don't want to wrestle around in the mud or sand, or in a bamboo stand, wasting time and compromising the mission you are on.

War is never a pretty thing. War is brutal, tough, and bloody. War is unforgiving. War is hell, and you will have hell to pay if you forget that for even one second. You'll never get a second chance to kill your enemy, should you respect him enough to let him walk away, as our contemporary American society seems to believe. Americans today are not as tough or committed to victory over Al-Qaeda as my great-uncle Ernie Simpson's generation was committed to victory over Nazi Germany and Imperial Japan. The Greatest Generation remains just that, for they came together like no other to sacrifice, struggle, and prevail. They did not need to conceptualize words like *unity*, *valor*, or *will*; they lived them, and because they lived them, we enjoy the freedoms we have today as Americans. We are facing an enemy today in Al-Qaeda that has proven it enjoys denying Americans their freedoms, including the fundamental right to breathe safely on American soil.

Al-Qaeda, the enemy that American culture is forcing us to respect, did not show any respect or remorse for the three thousand people murdered in cold blood on American soil on September 11th. They took pride in their vicious and diabolical attack, just as they took pride in the beheadings of American citizens Daniel Pearl and Nicholas Berg. So why should we show Al-Qaeda any respect at all?

*Death to Al-Qaeda.*

I say we should drop Al-Qaeda terrorists from trapdoors in the cargo holds of jet passenger planes, from 35,000 feet, midway over the North Atlantic between America and Europe. And tell them to enjoy the view on the way down.

Generosity is a good trait, and we should be generous to the killer whales and the great white sharks in the ocean, and give said marine life a few free lunches. Call it charity. Each time we strike and kill an Al-Qaeda cell, remember every American who was murdered in cold blood by Al-Qaeda on September 11th.

To hell with the politically correct bullshit that is all too prevalent in American society today. It has weakened our warrior spirit and has become a serious impediment to victory over Al-Qaeda. For instance, I heard from Marines in Fallujah in late February 2004 that we paratroopers were too aggressive; the Marines didn't think this was the answer to winning the guerrilla war in Western Iraq. The leadership of the U.S. Marines had the bright idea to come in with a softer approach, to creep in like fog. However, as Mike Tucker noted in a field intelligence analysis on Western Iraq to the 1st Marine Expeditionary Force in mid-February 2004, as the Marines were preparing to take over command in Fallujah, "If you think that not killing your enemy in Fallujah is the answer, then you and your men are in for a world of hurt." Which, unfortunately, came true.

No matter how hard you try, war will never change.

As you can see in Afghanistan, they have been at war for centuries and it will always be that way, and all the money and reconstruction aid will not change the thought process of the Taliban one bit. The Taliban are who they are: stone-cold evil Islamic fascists intent on murdering Americans left, right, and center (and happy to behead Afghan women for the crime of walking to a market alone), and killing is all they understand.

Killing the Taliban is essential to victory in Afghanistan. Eliminating the Taliban and Al-Qaeda's safe havens in Pakistan, moreover, is crucial if we hope to achieve global victory over Al-Qaeda.

To defeat the enemy, you must become the enemy. Don't get me wrong; I'm not saying that to defeat the Taliban we must become stone-cold evil Islamic fascists. I'm not saying that at all. One thing to understand is that to win in war, you must become war. That's just the nature of the beast. And in any war, as Sun Tzu stated thousands of years ago, in order to defeat your enemy, you must know your enemy. To defeat our enemies in Afghanistan, we must become fluent in the languages of Afghanistan, the culture of Afghanistan, and the history of Afghanistan. Only this way can we use our enemy's tactics, language, culture, and history against him.

Only a guerrilla warrior can defeat a guerrilla in a guerrilla war. Bureaucrats don't win wars, and neither do lawyers, diplomats, or reconstruction aid specialists. Warriors and spies win wars. That was true in Sun Tzu's time, in Alexander's time, in Patton's time, and that remains true in our time, and will for all time.

Speak to the Taliban and Al-Qaeda and all radical Islamic terrorists in the only language they understand, which is called the flight path of the 7.62mm bullet, and the language of rifle, sidearm, grenade, mortar, and knife. With all the fat cats' opinions out there, coming from people who have never seen action and will never see action, my opinion is probably one of the most accurate, seeing that I've been face-to-face with the Taliban in Afghanistan and with Al-Qaeda in the Near East and Central Asia. Like my brother Rangers and snipers and all who have bled in this war, I have walked the terrain of which I speak.

Victory against our enemies, in the war of survival which we are fighting against Al-Qaeda and the Taliban and their allies, worldwide, will only come with daring, strength and guile, ruthlessness, total commitment to killing our enemies, and employing deception and combat savvy at every opportunity. Which is no different, really, than the tactics, strategy, and philosophy of Alexander the Great in Afghanistan over two thousand years ago. As U.S. Army Specialist Sylas Carter, a combat infantryman of the 101st, said in Mosul, Northern Iraq, on November 8, 2003:

> Hemingway's dead-solid right about war—it's a street fight. War is a street fight, simply on another level. And the same rule applies: put the other guy down so that he stays down. If we lose the street fight in Iraq, all the glad-handing and politicking and money we've spent here won't amount to dust in the wind. We've gotta fight the street fight. All the way. Win the street fight, and you win this war.

And it was just as clear to me in Western Iraq that "it's all close-quarter battle now, in this war and in Afghanistan, CQB and Special Ops . . . the street fight here, the war here, it's all close-quarter battle . . . you really have to know your rifle, your knife, and your sidearm; that's what this war comes down to." I guess me and Sylas Carter and I have something in common. No one really listened to us, however. Bush has failed to win the street fight in Iraq because he failed to ever fight it in the first place, placing all his faith in money to win the war, not in American spies and warriors. And in my experience, that's what all war comes down to: You must never forget that the last man standing wins the war, and he only wins because he never forgets that war is a street fight, and the only dirty fight is the one you lose.

Alexander the Great was not politically correct, but he won because he did not show respect to those who did not deserve respect. Like the great Union Army general Ulysses S. Grant, Alexander the Great understood that war is war, and that to win a war, you have to fight a war.

We'd now been in Fallujah for over a month. The nights became cooler in early October, and the scent of fires was now drifting over the desert in the chill darkness. Volturno was being hit with mortars and rockets every night. The enemy's barrages would start around 6:30 P.M. and go on for an hour or so.

Now back 100 percent, operationally, my first priority was to be brought up to speed on what went down in the field over the past forty-eight hours, and all current intelligence. After being briefed by Sergeant First Class Lopez, I returned to my team's hootch to brief them on upcoming missions. By this time, we were pretty much acclimatized, but the daytime heat was still scorching.

Cooling out with my team on a mid-October day, I heard the gruff, bearlike roar of Lopez from out of nowhere. "LeBleu!" I rambled over to see what was up. A U.S. Army Special Forces major was standing with Lopez under camouflaged netting outside our Scouts' quarters. Lopez introduced me to the major, a tall, deeply tanned man with brown hair. He was wearing nonmilitary khaki trousers, a desert-colored shirt, and a vest. He was dressed very much like the Delta Force commandos I'd been on missions with in Fallujah. Like many men in Special Forces, he was reserved, self-contained, very quiet and calm. He held a long black rifle case in his left hand.

I remember thinking to myself, *It's good to see Special Forces, somebody from my old world in Special Ops, at our hootch.* We didn't salute, for in the Spec Ops community, you never salute in a war zone. The reason is simple: It gives the enemy the opportunity to kill higher-ranking people. It's a very bad habit while in combat— one that the regular U.S. military still hasn't learned to avoid.

"What's up, sir?" I said to the major.

"I've heard that you've seen quite a bit of action, and that you're the go-to sniper in this neck of the woods," he said.

"I guess so, sir," I said.

The major set the rifle case down on the ground between us and popped the latch on each end, opening it like a briefcase. He looked up at me and asked, "You ever had any time on one of these?"

I glanced down at the open case and saw a sniper rifle that I was fortunately familiar with: an SR-25 7.62 caliber sniper rifle. I'd fired the SR-25 on ranges, as a Ranger. It fires both semiautomatic and full automatic, like the old M16s. Inside the case, the rifle was, of course, broken down into the upper and lower receivers, the scope, eight 20-round magazines that held 118LR (Long Range), which were special ball ammunition of 7.62 caliber, bipod legs, and a silencer stamped U.S. NAVY. (The SR-25 is a preferred sniper rifle of U.S. Navy SEALS and common to all U.S. Special Operations Forces.)

I looked at the major, who was now standing up with his arms folded, and said, "Roger that, sir."

The major nodded and replied, "We want you to try it out in the field and tell us what you think." You could tell he had to get going, and I thought again, *This guy is a real professional from my neck of the woods.*

"All right, sir," I said.

"Happy hunting," he said with a smile, and left.

I closed the case as Lopez smiled at me, saying, "You lucky fucker!" That was Lopez's favorite saying, in truth.

"I guess so, Sergeant," I said, shrugging my shoulders. I picked up the case and carried it to my hootch, to inspect and assemble the new rifle in my collection, which now consisted of the M24 sniper rifle, the .50 cal Barrett sniper rifle, and now, the new SR-25.

By mid-afternoon, I'd finished assembling my SR-25 and inspecting the rounds for any burrs on the bullets, or any other defects. A sniper must always inspect his bullets so that he knows he can rely on each of his rounds while in combat. The slightest defect on a bullet can drastically affect its flight path at long ranges.

Lopez called me again after I'd assembled my SR-25, to let me know that I'd be going out on a "leaders' recon" with 10th Mountain the next day. A leaders' recon is when key leaders go out on a mission, and usually includes a sniper team leader, a platoon leader (usually a lieutenant), a platoon sergeant, the platoon RTO, and squad leaders from that platoon. You're basically carrying out reconnaissance on routes, houses, and the objectives you plan on hitting.

Lopez briefed me that evening, saying, "Go link up with Captain Kirkpatrick at his hootch for timelines and details for the mission tomorrow."

I walked two miles around the man-made lake where Uday and Qusay Hussein had tossed in the corpses of tortured, raped, and murdered political prisoners during Saddam Hussein's dictatorship. The cool breeze that night rippled the surface of the dark lake waters, which held the skeletons of countless folks who had stood up to Saddam. Ironically enough, we called it Dreamland. We thought it was a good name for a lake in the middle of hell.

I made my way to the captain's quarters to meet with him face-to-face and let him know that I was 10th Mountain's sniper attachment for the leaders' recon and mission. The captain briefed me on time hacks—when to report the next morning (at 8:00 a.m.) for the operations order, which is basically a detailed briefing that explains every element of a mission. I noticed that he was a pretty short man, maybe five-foot-five at the most, and I hoped that he didn't have "Joe Pesci Syndrome." I find that many short guys suffer from this condition: a profound self-consciousness about being short that makes them cocky and tough in order to compensate for their lack of God-given height.

After talking with him, it was very clear that Captain Scott Kirkpatrick did not have Joe Pesci Syndrome. He was low-key, witty, hard-core, and very motivated, which no doubt came from his grueling regimen as a marathon runner. Tough as nails, he could run two miles in nearly nine minutes flat. He struck me as the kind of officer who treated you like a man, which was very rare in the military. You only see that kind of professionalism, generally speaking, in Spec Ops. Captain Kirkpatrick reminded me of the Spec Ops commanders I'd been around in the 1990s, with his calmness, professionalism, and straight-up, solid combat officer's personality.

After the mission details were clear, we shook hands and I said, "I'll see you bright and early in the morning, sir."

As I headed back along the lakeshore, I heard mortar tubes thumping off in the distance. This meant just one thing: *Run!* Within seconds, it was raining mortars on Volturno. I hauled ass to the cover of date palms and scrub brush and blocks of concrete rubble, trying to time when to move by the impacts of the mortar rounds. Dashing from tree to tree, I made it back to the Scouts' hootch. I remember breathing heavily as I walked in, saying, between gasps, "Looks like it's raining again." The Scouts asked me where I'd been and I told them about my meeting with Captain Kirkpatrick.

Once the mortars had stopped, I gathered everyone together and gave a quick class on the SR-25, regarding effective range, how many rounds it held (20-round magazine), and the stopping power of the ammunition.

Late in the night, I briefed my team, Eggleston and Arroyo, about the leaders' recon in the morning. "It's just a leaders' recon," I said, "so I'll be going alone. Martin will be going, and Robi will drive us." Robi, otherwise known as Specialist Wesley Robison from Utah, was about five-foot-nine, dark-haired, tanned and slim, and he wore black plastic glasses. A former paramedic in civilian life, Robi flooded the hootch with his '50s doo-wop music. We all gave him hell for this—the kind of teasing British folks call "taking the piss out of you"—but he took it in stride.

We all went to our cots and everyone racked out for the night, except for me. I stayed up to prep my field intelligence and dope for the SR-25 sniper rifle. Going over the infiltration route on my map of Fallujah, I made sure that I had every single detail down, refreshing my memory with measurements on everything that was specific to terrorists and insurgents in Fallujah. I memorized the route of the leaders' recon, eyeballing the area between the southern edges of the city and the Euphrates River. I'd heard of this place before; called "the Boneyard," it was filled with looted, stripped-down buildings that from a distance looked like whalebones and dinosaur skeletons. High green seas of saw grass jutted along both shores of the Euphrates, beyond the Boneyard, and water buffalo grazed in swampy grass fields nearby.

The Boneyard was a strange, ghosted place. It was a bare, eerie, wasteland of looted factories. There were a few villages in close proximity, and along with the water buffalo, you'd see donkeys and goats meandering about. Oddly, you'd often see dead goats near a dam south of the Boneyard, on both sides of a concrete bridge spanning the Euphrates.

Before I crashed that night, I slipped my map into the left cargo pocket of my desert bottoms and walked outside, staring at the night sky. I was mentally preparing myself to be back in combat, even though I knew it was only a leaders' recon. I remember telling myself, "Here we go. Round two, back into the eye of the hurricane."

I had to be at Captain Kirkpatrick's hootch at eight, and I wasn't much of a breakfast person, especially with the scent of sewage choking me in the gray early morning. Not being much of a coffee drinker, the morning aroma of the desert was my cup of joe. Hey, I'm grateful for such gifts as that fragrant aroma of Fallujah—an absolutely righteous scent indeed. Reminded me that I was still alive. Sans java, I went over to Martin's hootch at the Scouts and told him, "Grab Robi and let's roll."

Martin said, "Okay," then yelled, "Robi, get your shit—we're going," and we headed to the Humvee. I jumped in the back with my SR-25 and a 20-round magazine of 7.62x51mm 118LR jacked in, and two other magazines. I also carried my sidearm with three 15-round magazines. I wanted to be in the back so that I could have sufficient elevation to scan in front of our Humvee and our convoy.

Martin rode shotgun as Robi took the wheel, setting his M4 to the right side, a lesson learned from our first ambush in early September. I was alone in the back. It was terribly hot, a choking heat, with brilliant blue skies on all horizon lines. The mirage was heavy that day. I banged on the plywood and said, "Let's roll." We moved out toward 10th Mountain's command post, linked up with Captain

Kirkpatrick, and went over last-minute details on the reconnaissance route, making sure everybody was on the same page. His last words at the briefing before we mounted up in the Humvees were, "Everybody be careful out there." Captain Kirkpatrick was cool and professional as always; in truth, he was the best company commander I saw in combat in Iraq.

We headed outside the wire, moving toward the city, and started our reconnaissance on dirt roads away from the Cloverleaf. Going down these dirt roads, just as I did during all missions in Fallujah, I remember taking more mental pictures, a sort of personal "photographic" field intelligence, marking key mosques and buildings in my memory. As with most missions, you could feel the apprehension in the air, but on this particular morning, the tension was as heavy as the smoke and the ever-present stench of goat manure and sewage.

The locals gave us hate stares and seemed especially distant. The usual aromas in the air were thicker that morning, more potent than usual. One strange thing I'd noticed is that right before we'd get hit, the smells usually became much stronger the deeper we'd get into Fallujah. By this time, I'd gained what most combat vets refer to as "the sixth sense." Once you've seen significant action, you can tell when something is wrong or when something is about to happen in combat. I had that same feeling now that I'd had in the Rangers before coming under fire—a certain feeling in my gut right before being ambushed.

I began shouting back and forth with Martin when I'd see a pile of trash or a group of suspicious people on a corner, and he'd respond, "I got it." I remember thinking to myself how strangely everyone was acting and how empty the streets and alleys were, key indicators for a fight. Robi was quiet and cool behind the wheel. Maybe Utah was on his mind, who knows, or he may have been hearing a Frankie Valli song; nonetheless, he was solid, eyes on, with his head in the game.

We started rolling northwest for the Boneyard, skirting the southern edges of Fallujah, dust trailing behind us. We were second in the convoy, following a 10th Mountain Humvee with a .50 cal mounted. Our trail Humvee was mounted with a MK19 40mm grenade launcher. One thing about 10th Mountain that impressed me: They were always loaded for bear. Their light infantrymen never hesitated to carry shotguns in Fallujah, for instance, which are ideal weapons for guerrilla warfare in jungle terrain and on urban turf in a desert environment, such as the tight alleys and jammed streets of Fallujah.

Sweat was pouring, and I remember thinking, *I hope we're not out here too much longer because I didn't bring any water*. By this point, I'd been training my body to survive for long periods of time in the desert without water. But this mission was extremely hot. We snaked back onto the main dirt road leading to the Boneyard, away from the mud huts and concrete villas that we'd just passed. As we started to pull away from the village on the main dirt road, I scanned ahead through the clouds of dust to ensure we were still on our route. Perhaps 500 meters west, a white pickup truck approached from the south, rolling slowly through crowds on both sides of a dirt road, heading north.

The lead 10th Mountain Humvee, with "Ma Deuce," the M2 .50-caliber heavy machine gun on point, now pulled ahead of us, at least 50 meters, making a huge gap in the convoy. I shouted, "Close the gap!" and Robi punched it. The next thing I knew, all was blackness and smoke and my ears were ringing and I remember the back of the Humvee lifting up off of the ground, throwing me to the front of the bed, and slamming me into Martin's back. Somehow I pulled myself together quickly, got my bearings, and dropped down, taking a knee in the back of the Humvee, dropping my chin to my chest as the shock and blast of the IED slammed the Humvee down on the dirt road, dust thick in the air.

Strangely enough, and quite fortunately, I knelt over my scope. I know of no reason why I did this, but I guess it was a gut feeling. One of my instincts was always, "If you protect your glass (scope), you will always be able to see your target."

My ears were ringing harder and louder than they had from any other IED blasts. This one felt ten times stronger. What seemed an eternity was probably only about thirty seconds, just enough time for me to get my bearings back. When I came to, I immediately started scanning 360 degrees, looking for a triggerman. By this point, I had learned from field intelligence that there would always be triggermen at least 300 meters from any IED ambush site. Once I'd completed my quick 360-degree scan, I turned to my team, to make sure they weren't wounded or dead.

I was looking through the black smoke rising around the rest of the convoy behind me. At that time, I'd seen a massive crater—I remember thinking, *A Humvee could fit in this crater*—and that's when we found out that there were three daisy-chained 155mm artillery rounds in the IED that had damn near killed us. At this point in the Iraq War, the insurgents were becoming more clever with how they were emplacing IEDs; for instance, in this ambush, they'd dug into the road itself, placed the IED, and then repaved the road, to the point where it looked like any normal road in Fallujah. This was a very different tactic than they'd used previously, where they'd just placed IEDs in trash on the side of roads, camouflaged with burlap sacks and rocks, or inside the carcass of a dead horse, dog, or donkey (even inside human corpses).

The radio was hot with calls for accountability: "Get a status report, get a status report!" was coming over our radio in the Humvee. We noticed crowds building up and people on rooftops behind us, in the village we'd just passed, some 300 meters to our rear. By this time, the lead 10th Mountain vehicle had turned around and was hauling ass to get back and help us.

We turned the whole convoy around and quickly got into a herringbone formation. Now the former trail Humvee with the Mark 19 became the lead vehicle, on point for the convoy, and the .50 cal mounted Humvee became trail vehicle, on rear guard for the convoy.

We'd maneuvered ourselves to the left side of the road so that the MK19's fields of fire were covering us. We did this so that I could maintain a direct line of sight west down the road, with my SR-25 set up on its bipod legs on top of the platform above the cab of the Humvee. The crowd was west of us, roughly 300 meters up ahead, and moving toward us. Now I could see a white pickup truck rolling away from the crowd, heading north. Scoping the truck, scanning now, I could see the wooden handgrips of AK-47 Kalashnikov assault rifles carried by men in dark *dishdashas* in the bed of the white truck.

*Insurgents.*

I yelled to the MK19 gunner in the lead vehicle, "Take out that white truck! Shoot the white truck—it's getting away!"

The MK19 gunner from 10th Mountain did not fire.

A 10th Mountain sergeant ran up to the gunner and started chewing his ass, saying, "What the fuck is wrong with you! Why didn't you shoot that truck?"

The gunner was frozen on the MK19, staring into space, his hands wrapped around the triggers. He didn't reply. The sergeant grimaced and pointed left, to a field south of us, and shouted, "Fire your goddamn weapon!"

The gunner fired two rounds from the MK19, into the open farmer's field, in front of a small mud house. The sergeant glared at the gunner and said, "Now you know how to pull the fuckin' trigger! Get back on point. If you see that fuckin' white pickup truck again, you had better fuckin' ventilate the motherfucker!"

The gunner looked down, morose and with eyes downcast, and muttered, "Roger, Sergeant."

*What the fuck was that?* I said to myself. I turned to Martin, laughing. "I think 10th Mountain just did a live-fire test fire."

I remember thinking, *Why haven't we taken AK fire yet?* This was standard operating procedure for IED ambushes in Fallujah. I said to Martin, "Don't you think it's weird that we haven't taken fire yet?" He raised his eyebrows, wincing, and said, "Yeah, it *is* weird," as he scanned the rooftops around us.

The crowd to the west had become a rolling mob. It had surged fast, and the road was full of Iraqis moving slowly toward us, dust boiling up all over the street. Some of the men had their faces and heads completely covered by black *khaffiyehs*; others wore red *khaffi-yehs*, wrapped ninja-style around their heads, with only their eyes showing through my scope. For a split second, I thought, *Fuckin' Mogadishu all over again*, remembering what my brothers went through in Somalia on October 3, 1993, and the waves of mobs that had killed Shughart and Gordon when they saved Durant's life.

I dialed the dope into my scope at 300 meters, preparing for a shot. Looking through my scope, I called out to a 10th Mountain officer, whom I'd just seen out of the corner of my eye. "We've got a pretty big crowd building 300 meters west," I said. The officer was hustling down the right side of our convoy, headed right for me. He looked at the mob as I looked through my scope, my SR-25 set up on its bipods, resting on the plywood. I could feel his reluctance and thought, *This guy's hesitating when there is no time to hesitate.* At that second, I made the call.

"Check it out, sir. I can put a round at the edge of a building at the end of the street, at the corner, which will spray concrete in the direction of the crowd, all over their faces. That will push them back."

He looked at me quizzically and replied, "You can do that?"

"Roger," I said.

"Do it," he said.

I yelled to Robi, "Kill the engine!" Our Humvee was still set in, with the engine running hard, and as I looked through my scope, the vibration was throwing off my shot, shaking my rifle. Once the engine was quiet, I got back in a firing position, my right cheek resting on the stock, and eyed the crowd through my scope. I took a deep breath—your first breath is always your relaxation breath, to calm you—and exhaled slowly, feeling myself calm down from the adrenaline rush of the IED ambush. As I took my second breath and started to exhale, I zeroed in on a crack that I could see, running dark and jagged down the brown-painted concrete wall. I began to slowly squeeze my trigger, sending a round to that exact spot of the corner of the building closest to the mob.

Concrete sprayed across the crowd.

The crowd began to disperse, running in all directions. The street was clear now. Mogadishu came to mind again. *We aren't going down like that today; no fucking way.*

I did my follow-through—keeping the trigger to the rear, I kept my sight alignment on the target, ensuring my round had hit exactly where I'd wanted it to—and then I closed my mouth and ground my teeth, feeling a sense of joy that my idea had actually worked. I'd removed the mob's threat against the convoy without killing a single person.

I looked over to the 10th Mountain lieutenant, who said, "Holy shit! Nice shot!"

"We've still got movement around those buildings and rooftops to our right, 300 meters away," I said, and he replied, "Roger." He walked over to the lead vehicle, to inform them of the enemy movement, and at that time the MK19 gunner swiveled around, facing northwest toward the rooftops.

Perhaps a minute passed and then all hell broke loose. AK-47s opened up from rooftops, alleys, and street corners, hammering us from all compass points. It was like a boxing match, I remember thinking, and we were going toe-to-toe with the enemy. For once in Iraq, the insurgents had decided to trade hooks and uppercuts with us.

We weren't moving and they weren't running away. Walls of fire were rolling in both directions, and 10th Mountain soldiers were yelling, "Where the hell is it coming from?" as they returned fire, scoping the rooftops. I knew we could not remain without the high ground for long, without becoming sitting ducks. A fundamental law of war: He who holds the high ground wins the fight.

We were surrounded by 7.62 caliber rounds, cracking by us, flying over us, and hitting the street. I took a low knee in the back of the Humvee, ducking down and then peeking up, zeroing in on muzzle flashes on the rooftops. I looked over at Martin and said, "Hey, Martin, we're getting fired at now!"

"No shit!" he shouted back, grinning with the little smirk he had whenever we were under fire.

I could see a yellow heavy-equipment crane, missing its tracks, about 100 meters northwest of us. *If I can get to that crane, I can set up and start taking out the enemy,* I thought, *so the infantry squads can advance to the dirt berm.* The berm was 50 meters west of the crane, in front of it. I knew that if I could get to the crane, 10th Mountain would follow; we'd be closer to the enemy, making it easier for us to strike and kill the insurgents.

I kept ducking and rising, trying to locate the enemy and get a better feel for potential cover near the crane. Nobody had advanced yet; nobody had moved toward the enemy. Luckily for us, the enemy couldn't shoot for shit, but their fire was still heavy over and around us, AK rounds pinging off Humvees and striking sand and rocks, dust trails zinging off the dirt road.

*Make it to the crane,* I thought, *make it to the crane.*

I knew it was risky, given that it was a 100-meter dash with no cover in between. You're never supposed to be up for more than three seconds when you're under fire. The saying goes, "I'm up, he sees me, I'm down." All American infantry are trained to rush for three seconds under fire, then roll or take cover, and then move again, in a pattern of three-second rushes, until you can find cover or you have reached the objective. This is also true for special operations. What a lot of people in combat tend to forget is that if you can see the enemy, the enemy can see you. Nobody's invincible. As bold as many of us think we are, the bottom line is that nobody is Superman in war.

But every so often you have to go for broke. Trusting your instincts means that sometimes, you have to take a real risk. The plain damn fact was, I knew that the crane would provide ideal cover to kill the enemy, and the only way to get there was to haul ass, hell for leather. For a split second, I remember telling myself, *Should've brought more water!*

I ducked down and yelled to Robi, "Stay here; stay behind cover."

In his usual low-key tone, he said, "Roger."

"Hey, Robi," I said, and he looked at me. "You want to see something crazy?" I looked at him, said "Watch this!", and leapt over the side of the Humvee with my rifle in my right hand and a small field radio tucked into my vest. I landed on both feet as the enemy fire increased, kicking up rounds in the dirt around me. I sprinted fast and hard, running first at about a 30-degree angle north and then aiming straight for the crane.

I could hear enemy fire all around me, and the shouts of 10th Mountain soldiers behind me. I remember thinking, *Damn, it's hot*. Soaked with sweat, I was closing in on the crane, Kalashnikov fire cracking next to me. I have never run faster in my life.

Somehow, by the grace of God, I made it. I got down behind the back side of the crane, breathing heavily, trying to catch my breath. I took one deep breath and let it out, trying to calm myself down. I got into the prone and crawled underneath the crane so that I'd have cover above me. As I was lying under the crane, I realized I didn't have good-enough elevation to engage the rooftops. Since the tracks were off the wheels of the crane, I wedged myself between the body and the top of the track—I was laying on the left wheel. Steel surrounded me. I could hear bullets hitting the crane, pinging and ricocheting in all directions.

Now I had a better line of sight to start engaging the enemy on the rooftops. I fired three rounds, rapidly, on semiautomatic, at an insurgent on a rooftop who was firing an AK-47. He disappeared with my last round. I don't know if I killed him, but right away, the fire stopped from that rooftop. I knew it was crucial now for 10th Mountain infantrymen to push up toward my position and begin engaging the enemy. Tenth Mountain was with my Ranger brothers in Mogadishu and they were with me now in Fallujah.

I grabbed my radio, called in my location at the crane, and told them that they were good, now, to push forward up to the dirt berm, roughly 50 meters in front of me.

"Roger," said the 10th Mountain RTO.

I don't know which RTO it was; it may have been Specialist Patrick Lybert, twenty-five, from Ladysmith, Wisconsin, who was killed in action on June 21, 2006, fighting against the Taliban in

Afghanistan. (At the time of his death in Afghanistan, Lybert was a squad leader and a staff sergeant.)

I thought it would be best for me to stay put, and keep scanning for—and killing more—enemy. I stayed under the crane, snug between the wheel and the body, as enemy rounds continued slamming into the crane, thudding off the metal in an odd rhythm: first, a few would hit, equally spaced, followed by a barrage of bullets hitting the crane all at once. I said out loud to myself, "I'll stay here until I can hear 10th Mountain coming up, from the rear." Tenth Mountain knew that I was somewhere around the crane, but they didn't know exactly where I was, in my cover, within the crane. I heard them approaching, what seemed to be a squad of infantry. Before I knew it they had passed the crane, moving quickly to the dirt berm. Once they had pushed in front of me and were on the berm, I dropped my barrel down so that I wouldn't be pointing at their backs.

I located and grabbed my three expended brass because first, a sniper should never shoot more than three rounds from one position. And second, you should never leave brass in combat as a sniper, in order to prevent the enemy from counter-tracking you. I tucked the three expended brass into a small pocket I'd made on the left forearm sleeve of my blouse. I slipped out of my cover and got under the crane, then slid out backwards, keeping the crane between me and the enemy.

Coming out on one knee, I switched radio channels to the Scout frequency and called Martin. "Do you see the dirt berm at your two o'clock? Meet me there."

"Roger," he replied.

I tucked my radio away back on my vest now and hustled up, moving out quickly around the right side of the crane, heading up to the berm to the 10th Mountain squad. Strangely, the enemy fire had stopped for a moment. Then, just a few seconds later, fire came down on us again as soldiers were moving, taking cover, and trying to locate the insurgents. Enemy fire slowed to pop shots, and the 10th Mountain soldiers were carefully selecting targets, wisely conserving ammunition.

We had no idea, really, of what to expect, as happens all too often in combat. Turns out we were an hour into what proved to be a three-hour firefight.

As I ran up to the berm, I noticed there were 10th Mountain light infantrymen in the prone all across the berm. I realized I didn't want to be at either end of the squad, because that would make me stand out to the enemy. As a sniper, you always want to blend into your surroundings; in this case, it was an infantry squad, and I wanted to make myself as inconspicuous as possible—as if I was indeed one of them, a grunt with a rifle, returning fire.

I saw an opening on the right side of the squad, toward the end of their line of soldiers, and I set up next to a rifleman who was firing on single shot, engaging the enemy on the rooftops with his M4.

"Don't get too carried away; only shoot what you can hit," I said to him as I scoped the rooftops. The truth is, if you let an infantryman keep shooting, he will. Privates, especially, rarely think about conserving ammunition.

I did a quick scan of my surroundings and saw a gray concrete building in front of me and more buildings off to the left.

There were minarets of mosques far off in the distance, toward downtown Fallujah, and I could see a paved road in the distance, running north-south. I knew the road was quite a fair stretch, but didn't know exactly how far away at that very moment. Everything was going down quickly, and I was anxious for Martin to show up and spot for me. Enemy fire was sporadic, at this point, and 10th Mountain soldiers continued to return fire.

More and more soldiers began to arrive and throw down on the enemy, slowly turning our hasty fighting position into a defensive perimeter. Within seconds, Martin arrived, out of breath and gasping, but on the case.

"You're a crazy motherfucker, you know that?"

"That's what I keep hearing," I replied.

I immediately pointed out the road to Martin and remember saying, "If anything comes our way, that road is going to be a key avenue of approach. That road needs to be our main focus."

Fallujah insurgents were using pickup trucks as gun platforms, which Al-Qaeda and Somali rebels in Mogadishu had done in 1993, and which we'd been briefed on in Iraq, on many occasions. We were all aware of the fact that insurgents and terrorists in Iraq often mounted heavy machine guns on pickup trucks, thus turning them into gun trucks.

Martin agreed, shouting to a 10th Mountain platoon leader, "Hey, sir, be aware of that road!" Martin turned back around now, staring at the road, his eyes fixed on a far distant point perhaps 800 meters away.

I said to him, "Some leaders' recon," thinking that you're never supposed to make contact on any kind of reconnaissance, and of course, we had most definitely made contact and remained engaged.

He smirked and replied, "No shit, huh."

Enemy fire kept rolling, the rounds kicking up dust and sand around us and 10th Mountain. My main concern now was the road, and my intent was to do everything possible as a sniper to keep the enemy from advancing on us, using that road to kill us and 10th Mountain. I remained the only sniper on the ground, with 10th Mountain, at this point. Because this was supposed to be a leaders' recon, no other snipers had been attached to 10th Mountain on this day. Moreover, because this was a leaders' recon, we had no spotting scope or any binoculars to see past my Leupold 10x fixed scope on my SR-25. Fortunately, my Leupold was solid, and with it, I could see out to 1,500 meters; at 200 meters, I could see someone's eyelashes. But we had no spotting scope, which I remembered thinking would be a key lesson learned, if we survived that day.

Martin only had an ACOG 4x32 scope, a normal scope on his M4. You can see out to 800 meters through that scope, and it has tritium to illuminate its reticules at night. There was a saying for the Ranger battalion, when new equipment like the ACOG would come out in the army in the late 1990s: "Give it to the Rangers; if they can't break it, it's good." We Rangers were known for destroying an objective to the point where there was nothing left standing, and for testing new equipment to its maximum durability.

In the prone, looking through my scope, I said to Martin, "We need to figure out a distance to that road, so I can start putting my dope together in case I need to take a shot."

Martin, of course, was also a sniper team leader; in that way, it was quite fortunate he was my "Johnny on the Spot" acting, ad hoc spotter, because we'd both graduated from the U.S. Army Sniper School at Fort Benning.

Without spotting scope and binoculars, I had to rely solely on my range-estimation training from Sniper School. I knew, off the top of my head, that in open, flat desert terrain, you tend to underestimate your target distance. I factored that in and "guesstimated" the distance to the road.

A strange quiet descended all around us, and the 10th Mountain soldiers on the berm began changing magazines and drinking water. Everyone's uniform was dark with sweat and we were all red-faced and baked from the desert sun. The chain of command was rocking: Fire team leaders were checking rounds and water on each soldier and the light machine gunners were reporting to their fire team leaders, who then reported up to their squad leaders. You could hear grunts saying, "Fuck these insurgent motherfuckers!"

Staying in the prone, and figuring out the distance to the road, I heard from my left, "LeBleu!" I picked up my sniper rifle and sprinted over, peeling off left from the berm and hustling over toward my seven o'clock. I took a knee next to a 10th Mountain soldier firing an M4/M203. I nodded to him and he nodded back, sucking water from a hose connected to the Camel Bak water pouch on his back. He looked kind of wiped out, but his eyes were hard; he still had a lot of fight in him.

Kneeling, I began scanning from south to west, looking over the desert and mud huts far on the horizon. As I was scoping the desert, the soldier eyed the scope on his M4, leaning forward, looking south.

"There's a guy on a red motorcycle coming up the road," he said excitedly, all in one breath.

"That's the fuckin' triggerman for the IED," I said.

I knew that previous IED ambushes in Fallujah had been set off by one or two men on motorcycles. Turning right, I scoped the road and could see the man on the red motorcycle, with a red *khaffiyeh* wrapped turban-style around his head, wearing a white *dishdasha*, otherwise known as a "man dress." I was looking closely at him, searching for a cell phone, a weapon or a package—anything out of the ordinary.

He was about 75 meters away, approaching the crowd west of us, and at that moment, I thought, *He's more than likely headed into Fallujah*. I told the 10th Mountain soldier, "He's got nothing on him," and then I heard my name shouted from the berm. I could tell it was Martin. I sprang up and sprinted back to the berm. As I approached, someone from 10th Mountain began shouting, "That's the white truck—that's the fuckin' white truck!"

I realized in the middle of running back to the berm that it was no doubt the same white pickup truck we'd seen at the beginning of the IED ambush. As I dashed over to Martin, I was already preparing myself for a shot, thinking of range and the wind—I was damn glad that there was no wind that day. I hit the berm on my left shoulder and rolled over sideways, kind of submarining myself into the dirt berm—not exactly in the prone and certainly, not in the solid, correct firing position that I would've liked to line up a long-range shot. Sweat burned down my face.

I set my elevation to 800 meters on my Leupold scope, thinking that if need be, I could use Kentucky windage to line up the shot. There was no time to get into a better firing position. I could see the truck now through my scope, traveling from south to north, at what I guessed to be between 20 and 25 miles an hour. I could see that he was headed toward a factory located at least a mile north of his position, in the Boneyard. I knew that once he got inside the factory grounds, not only would I lose the shot, but it was also likely he'd grab more insurgents and load up the bed of that pickup with more AK-47s, and perhaps a heavy machine gun and RPGs.

Looking through my scope, I could see four insurgents with AK-47s held between their legs in the bed of the pickup, and a driver and passenger up front. I had chosen as my target an insurgent who was standing all the way up in the back of the truck, a big, broad-shouldered man. He was leaning forward slightly against the cab, a curved banana clip jammed in the AK, the wooden stock of the Kalashnikov up against his right shoulder, ready to fire. Ideally, you want to take out the wheelman, stopping the vehicle all together, if not causing an accident. Unfortunately, I didn't have that option available to me.

While I was tracking the white pickup, I said to Martin, "Act as my spotter on this."

"Yeah, I got you."

Martin looked through his ACOG on his M4. I gave him my reading and elevation setting, all at once, saying, "Eight hundred, no wind."

"Okay."

At that second, a 10th Mountain platoon leader shouted, "Does anyone have a shot on that white truck?"

I realized that not only did I have the shot, but I was also the only person on the berm with a weapon that could reach the white pickup truck. The light machine guns on the berm, known as M249 SAWs (Squad Automatic Weapons), could reach 800 meters, but had proven in combat in Iraq to be much more effective up to 600 meters.

I yelled out, "I've got it," and I heard, "Take the shot."

That's all I needed to hear.

I was tracking the white pickup truck the whole time and could see the sun reflecting off the barrels of their Kalashnikovs. The driver was wearing a white *dishdasha* and a grayish-white turban. The passenger wore a dark blouse with no *khaffiyeh*. He had short, greasy black hair. He looked fairly young, perhaps in his late teens. Two insurgents were squatting down in the bed of the pickup, near the tailgate. They wore dark *dishdashas* and their barrels were sticking straight up from between their legs.

Bore-sighted now, I could see sunlight gleaming off their muzzles. My target was clad in a dark shirt and gray trousers, and also wore no headdress. He had his right hand on the trigger of his AK, the Kalashnikov still shouldered, at the ready. I could see the wavy, dark grains in the wood of his stock. To his left, an insurgent was in a black *dishdasha*, his AK now disappeared within his man dress, his left hand jammed into his body. I remember thinking, *None of them are wearing headdresses*, filing that fact away into my dope for Fallujah, a key bit of field intelligence.

I knew that with the pickup moving at roughly 20 to 25 miles per hour, I'd have to give significant lead on the shot. I led it by one mil dot, which is more than your average lead in combat.

"Give it daylight," Martin said calmly, which is shorthand in sniper language, meaning, "Give it enough lead, lead the target." I took a very quick relaxation breath, because I was still breathing hard from the mad dash back to the berm, and feeling very rushed, I said quickly to Martin, "Taking the shot."

"Send it," Martin replied.

With my index finger on the trigger, the metal touching the meaty portion between the tip and first bone joint, I slowly but steadily pulled the trigger to the rear. Conscious of my breathing and exhaling slowly, I pulled the trigger, sending my first round toward the pickup. *Round fired.* I saw dirt kick up just before the road, and I realized I was quite short. The white pickup rolled on, not changing speed; no one in the bed of the pickup even looked at the spot where my round had hit the sand.

At least 200 meters short, I reckoned, watching the dust fall from the short round.

Martin said, "Short, right in front of the road."

I replied, "Roger."

*Holy shit, how far away is this?* I thought. I knew that it was considerably more than 800 meters now. The pickup truck was easily halfway to the looted factory in the Boneyard, insurgents in the back, their rifles held close to them. I was still zeroed in; I'd never taken my eye off the glass. My target continued to keep his Kalashnikov shouldered.

At that time, without looking, I reached up with my left hand to the elevation knob on my scope. I never took my eyes off my target, and still tracking the pickup, I twisted the knob a quarter turn.

Martin said, "One thousand meters."

"Sending second shot," I replied, keeping my right index finger on the trigger.

"Send it."

Taking in a quick breath, I started to exhale. Very slowly now, I applied pressure to the trigger, pulling it back, and I sent my second shot. I kept my follow-through, holding my trigger to the rear now, following the pickup through the scope. I saw the round hit the insurgent below the stock of his rifle, about midsection, on his right side. He dropped and fell backwards into the bed of the pickup, his Kalashnikov falling into the road.

"Hit," Martin replied in a conversational tone, calm and professional.

A 10th Mountain RTO to Martin's right shouted, "Holy shit, you got him! Fuckin' A!"

I didn't even know that the RTO was there. I reckon he'd been watching the entire action through his scope, during which only about five to six seconds had passed, even though it seemed much longer. Combat is strange that way; the smallest moments can turn into slow motion. There was a silence over all of us and then, we were taking fire again. Drop of a hat, it all went dead quiet.

Watching the white pickup through my scope, it seemed I'd surprised the other three insurgents in the back, as if I wasn't supposed to be able to reach them with one round from an American sniper rifle. As the American infantry proverb states, "One well-aimed round can change the course of combat." By now I could tell that the insurgents in the white pickup were surprised as hell. The two guys in the back, near the tailgate, dropped their AKs, as the third guy in the bed of the pickup quickly turned around and dove down. The pickup came to a screeching halt, dust kicking up all around it. They threw the dead insurgent over the driver's side onto the ground, where a pool of blood quickly formed.

The two remaining insurgents—carrying AK-47s and dressed in dark gray and black *dishdashas* but wearing no ninja-style *khaffi-yehs*—ran out of an alley and jumped into the bed of the pickup. I remember thinking of the fallen insurgent, *Is he really dead, or is he going to get up and run?* I kept eyeing his body through my scope. Everything was moving so fast now. I looked hard at his body to see if his chest was rising and falling, but it was motionless. After a few seconds had passed, it was clear to me that he was dead. At that same moment, the pickup hightailed it toward the factory.

"The pickup truck is speeding off," I said to Martin as I continued looking through my scope. Martin yelled back to 10th Mountain, "We got a hit, but two more guys jumped in the bed." The truck rolled hard, blowing past the factory, a huge cloud of dust following behind as it disappeared south. *Why the hell didn't 10th Mountain turn loose our .50 cal and MK19 on the pickup, right after I killed the insurgent?* Why did they let it get away? I'd marked the target. They had the range. This reflected a severe problem with our rules of engagement in the Iraq War, beyond May 1, 2003: Our grunts were being conditioned to fire only if fired upon first—giving battlefield initiative away to insurgents and terrorists—even though our rules of engagement clearly stated that when you see anyone carrying an AK-47 or any other weapon of war, deadly force is authorized.

The reality on the ground, however, was that once straight-up combat rules of engagement were rescinded by the Bush administration in May 2003, Department of Defense lawyers were all over Iraq, investigating grunts who were throwing down on insurgents and terrorists. Our infantrymen knew their careers were on the line anytime they pulled the trigger—which is not what you want a warrior thinking in the heat of battle.

Since no one in the white pickup truck had fired on 10th Mountain, our grunts hadn't fired back. As I lay there, in the prone, staying bore-sighted, I regretted this change in the rules of engagement. A well-known law of war says that once a sniper has marked an enemy vehicle—such as the white pickup carrying insurgents with AK-47s—all supporting heavy guns should light it up and destroy it. I made a mental note for my field Intel: *Remind grunts to kill the enemy once a sniper marks a target.*

Two women came out and dragged the body of the dead insurgent away, which happened quite often at war in Iraq—people always came out of nowhere and picked up dead insurgents. I would always refer to this phenomenon as "fighting ghosts," because the bodies were never left lying around. I assumed it was due to religious reasons, but it was extremely different and new to me. I was pissed off, thinking, "That was my kill, and they are taking it away from me!"

I glanced up to look at my elevation. It read 1,100 meters. *Holy shit, that was a long shot!*

I said to Martin, "That was eleven hundred meters."

"No shit," Martin said calmly.

I kept saying to myself, *I just got an eleven-hundred-meter confirmed kill, on a moving target*, over and over again, somewhat amazed that I'd made the shot.

"Good thing there was no wind," I said.

"Yep," Martin said, still looking through his spotting scope.

Martin came off his scope now, smiling at me, and said, "You lucky fucker."

"I don't know what you're talking about," I said, smiling, taking my eyes off my glass, too, and looking at him. I heard a 10th Mountain soldier behind me say, "Good job." There was still a strange quiet around us in the Boneyard.

I told Martin, "We need to get on one of those roofs so we can get eyes on everything—we need the high ground. Preferably, one of the rooftops facing south down the road." If the white pickup truck came back, we would have the advantage as long as we held the high ground.

As I was looking for a way up to the rooftops—there were no fire escapes or stairs—Martin yelled back to a 10th Mountain platoon leader, "Hey sir, we're gonna get on the rooftop so we can get eyes on that road, where the truck disappeared!" Martin grinned, looked at me, and said, "You ready?"

"Yeah."

"Let's go," he said as he got up. I picked up my sniper rifle. Both of us started to run from the berm to a two-story concrete building a little over 100 meters northwest from the berm. I was scanning the rooftops and alleys as we ran, saying to Martin, "You've got point," because he had the M4. As we got closer to the steel door of a nearby house, I collapsed down behind him so we were single file, very close together as we lined up against the wall of the house near a door.

Martin knocked. There was no need to do a dynamic entry if the homeowner would let us in. (A dynamic entry is an explosive entry which gains the advantage through violent, speedy action; for instance, by using a small explosive door charge to blast through a lock.) There was no other way to get to the roof—we had to go in through the door in order to get to the stairs that led to the roof. As the man answered the door, I pushed Martin in his back and said, "Go, go, go!"

Martin pushed the man to the right, into a room, as I banana-peeled left into a separate room, clearing it with my SR-25. I heard Martin yell, "Clear, I've got a family," and I replied, "All clear."

I hustled over to Martin and saw the whole family sitting on the floor. It was a big family, about seven people, including the grandparents. The man of the house was very big, very stocky, like a former wrestler who'd put on a potbelly. He and his family seemed calm, but you could see the nervousness in their eyes, wondering what we were doing in their house. I turned around to shut the front door, so no one could come in behind us. I could see concrete stairs in the center of the house, leading to the roof.

"I've got the roof," I said to Martin, and he filed in behind me as we went up the stairs. As we climbed, I felt for a hatch; I found one and opened it, and we hustled up to the concrete roof. I did a quick 360-degree scan, ensuring the roof was clear, before I came out on top of it. Yelling "Clear!" to Martin, I began to check out the roof, with Martin coming up behind me. I quickly moved to the south side of the roof, facing down the road, and set up in a kneeling position, behind a wall. The wall around the roof was about three feet high. It was very thick, in the way of many walls on Iraqi houses, where two- and three-foot-thick walls are not uncommon.

I was breathing heavily again, trying to get fresh air, and saying to myself, *Man, it's fuckin' hot!*

Martin stayed by the hatch, looking west toward the dirt berm and 10th Mountain, sending radio messages to them with our position and how we were set up. The man of the house came up on the rooftop now, and I looked back at Martin and yelled at the guy, "Go downstairs!" I jabbed with my free hand, pointing down. He was rambling in Arabic as he started walking toward me. "Does this motherfucker want to die?" I said under my breath.

Not only was he not complying with my commands, but he was also exposing my position for all to see by walking across the roof. I stood up quickly and pulled out my sidearm from my drop holster on my right hip, raising it toward him, and told him one last time, "Go downstairs!" He threw his hands up in the air, rambling again in Arabic, and began walking backwards quickly, toward the hatch.

I kept my front sight on his forehead, following him until he'd gone downstairs. As he descended the concrete steps back into his house, I holstered my sidearm and said to Martin, "He doesn't come back up those stairs again. If he comes back up those stairs again, he's dead." I did not have the time or the patience to explain to the Iraqi what we were doing on his roof. Martin nodded, looking west, not losing his fields of fire.

I hurried back over to my position, grabbed my sniper rifle, and backed off the wall so that my barrel was not sticking over the edge. I dropped my elevation down to 1,000 meters. The road was clear now, with no cars in sight. I was looking through my Leupold scope and could see clearly and accurately a little over 1,000 meters. I ripped my helmet off, tossing it in front of me against the wall, and rubbed the sweat from my forehead. I said to Martin, "Do you think any of these houses have a pool?" Martin just laughed, and said, "Yeah, no shit, I wish—California custom pools all around." The heat was just burning us, the sun a furnace in the cloudless sky. I asked Martin, "How much water did you bring for this leaders' recon?"

He replied, "I've got about half left in my Camel Bak, but it's all fucking hot," meaning he now had about one and a half quarts of water left in his pouch. I laughed. Martin always had to have fresh stuff; he wanted cold, iced water, not the desert-hot water in his Camel Bak, which most definitely did not taste fresh and cool! Martin had class, even at war.

"Well, that's just unfortunate, isn't it?" I said, smiling at Martin. "Maybe we can get on the horn and request some rooftop service, ice and cold beer and fresh water. Throw in a grilled steak with onions while you're at it. Apple pie and vanilla ice cream—why not? Little after-dinner coffee and brandy, and waitresses from Hooters."

We were now about two hours into the firefight, with small-arms fire still racing around. Some gunshots were still fairly close to us, and a lot of fire was sporadic throughout the city. I was still feeling strong, and realized that I'd only needed a few sips of water, just enough to wet my mouth.

A Quick Reaction Force Humvee rolled up to the house and combat-parked—sliding sideways—and I said to Martin, "QRF is here!"

"Hey, look at this," Martin said, and I turned around toward him. We could both see brass on the rooftops, sandbags, and paths leading from roof to roof, close enough where you could run and jump from house to house. We realized these were insurgent fighting positions and escape routes, running over 100 meters in all directions. I quickly gauged that not only were these insurgent fighting positions, but they also made perfect sites for IED triggermen to set off IED ambushes on Coalition convoys.

Martin said, "Let's check it out," and I nodded. I grabbed my sniper rifle and helmet and we hopped over to the first roof north of us, walking on a very thin, narrow pathway. We headed on north to the next roof. I could see bullet holes in the rambling concrete wall on the next roof, with a blood trail in the dust and dirt on the roof. I said to Martin, "Somebody was hit," and he nodded, looking east across the rooftops, scanning for enemy. I looked west down at the dirt berm and 10th Mountain, putting the puzzle together from the blood trail on the rooftop. It could have been the insurgent whom I'd shot three rounds at, from the crane; the line of sight matched where I'd shot from, perfectly.

The blood was dark purple, which means you've hit a main artery. In Sniper School, we were taught in combat tracking that the different colors of blood in a blood trail will pretty much tell you where you hit the enemy. For example, if you're tracking an enemy and you come across a light pink blood trail on a leaf, you more than likely have shot him in the chest area, perhaps in the lungs. On the other hand, if you come across a crimson-red blood trail, then you've likely hit him in a major vein or artery.

I could sit here all day and lay out the different ways and methods of tracking someone, but to keep from being counter-tracked (being followed), I always tried to keep it simple, by teaching Scouts and snipers that you will always know you're being tracked in the woods and in the jungle when you see a shadow. And in a city or any urban environment, you'll know you're being tailed by a reflection. As the saying goes, "In the woods, by shadow; in the city, by reflection; and in the desert, it would still be shadow."

Scent can also give you away when you're tracking or counter-tracking in the desert. Thanks to the advice of U.S. Special Operations, this was demonstrated accurately in the film *Spartan*, starring Val Kilmer. Cigarette smoke seems to travel miles in the desert; and a lit cigarette, pipe, or cigar can also be seen for miles in the desert.

The blood trail on the rooftop led east. "Let's follow it," I said to Martin.

As we began moving east, jumping from rooftop to rooftop, we saw a kid on one of the roofs, perhaps twelve years old. He was talking to us in Arabic and waving to us, as if he was going to show us the insurgents' escape routes across the rooftops. He wore a yellow shirt and dirty white trousers, with sandals on his dusty feet. He was kind of short, maybe four and a half feet tall, with dark black, greasy hair. There was dirt on his face, as if he'd been playing in the dirt before the ambush went off.

I motioned for him to come to me, to ensure that it was not a setup. He came within conversational distance of me and Martin.

I pointed down to the blood trail, and then gestured across the rooftops, pointing with my fingers down and waving my fingers in the international sign language for "walking." Seeing my gesture, the kid nodded and replied in Arabic, and waved for us to follow him. Now he was on point for me and Martin.

We followed the blood trail east by northeast, running across the rooftops. The blood trail patterns were all splotched out, near the adjoining walls of each rooftop, signaling that he was jumping as he was bleeding out, or perhaps that people were carrying him from roof to roof, and with each crossing, he was being jostled. As the kid showed us the secrets of the insurgent pathways, we noticed that the blood trail ended about 50 meters east, over a ledge, as if the insurgents had jumped down into the dirt. We didn't find a body or any blood at the base of the house, so it's quite possible the insurgents jumped into a vehicle and headed east into the heart of Fallujah.

As we sat on the last roof, taking a knee and looking at the ground, I remember thinking, *I give him an hour, tops.* The blood trail was thick, and clearly came from a fatal wound. "I guess we're back to fighting ghosts again," I said.

I didn't have anything to give to the kid for his help—no candy or cigarettes or chocolate—so I patted him on his back and gave him a thumbs-up, looking into his eyes. He smiled and gave me a thumbs-up in return, his coal-black eyes now bright. Martin grinned at him and said to me, "Let's head back." I could see in his eyes that he was thinking the same thing I was: We were all alone, at least 400 meters away from 10th Mountain, and we needed to get back now. Martin took point and the kid followed us, eventually running down into a stairwell that must have been his own house. We kept hustling back across the rooftops to get back to our first house, and when we got there, I saw immediately that the hatch was open.

Martin headed down with his weapon at the ready, his M4 shouldered. "Stairwell clear," he said. We rushed down the stairs into the house, which was fairly well lit by the sunlight that flooded in through the high windows. Martin went left and I went right, clearing the rooms again to ensure no enemy had snuck in on us. Martin yelled, "Clear!"

"Good," I replied. I could see the family was still seated together on a maroon rug with Turkish designs in it. There was a strong scent in the house of kerosene and very pungent body odor, mixed in with the smell of burning candles and incense. I remember thinking, *Wow, I can't believe this family stayed put the whole time*, because most Iraqi families will run the first chance they get, or turn on you. But they just sat there calmly, staring at us.

Martin headed toward the door. He opened it, looking both ways before he left the house. As he started to move, I trailed in behind him. Once outside the house, I could see the QRF Humvee and a tall captain standing next to it, with a full, wet, shiny CamelBak on his back. Martin kept heading toward the berm, and I broke left a little bit toward the captain, running up to the hose of his CamelBak on his right side, grabbed the hose without permission, and quickly sucked down two gulps of fresh, cool water. Invigorated by the drink, I winked at the captain and said, "Thank you, sir," and kept on running toward the berm. He didn't say anything, but I could feel his eyes on my back as I hustled back to the berm, as if he was thinking, "Who the hell was that!"

Back on the berm, I was nearly out of breath, thinking *It's too fuckin' hot out here.* I could see that the QRF was set up, four Humvees now emptying soldiers, as the firing stopped. Tenth Mountain prepared to leave, their soldiers climbing up in the Humvees, their rifles and machine guns outboard, the three-hour firefight now over. Martin and I stayed on the berm, pulling security for 10th Mountain as the Humvees' engines roared to life. Martin got on the horn to Robi, saying, "Get ready to roll!"

I could hear Robi's usual calm, even-toned voice replying, "Roger."

"What do you say we blow this taco stand?" I said to Martin. He laughed and said, "Hell yeah, sounds good to me." Martin being the TC, I told him to take off first and get in the Humvee, while I stayed, covering him with my sniper rifle. Once he got in the passenger's seat, I ran hard for the Humvee and jumped in the back, latching the tow strap in behind me. I shouted, exhausted, "We're good!"

The QRF waited for us to pull out in their perimeter, near the house we'd first entered. Once we began to roll east for Volturno, the QRF covered our six o'clock, on trail for the convoy. The ride back was smooth and uneventful, but make no mistake—everyone was still scanning for IEDs and any other signs of insurgents in the early dusk.

Riding back, I yelled up to Robi, "So was that crazy, or what?"

He smirked and shouted over the thudding heavy roar of the Humvee, "Yeah!" Robi was a man of few words, so getting even one word out of him was a real mission accomplished.

Coming up on the wire at Volturno, and drenched in sweat, I rested against the side of the Humvee and relaxed. I shouted up to

Martin, "See, you don't need any water!" He just shook his head. I was glad that I'd been trying to train my body to survive long periods of time without water in extreme conditions, because I'd just done exactly that. I'd passed my first test in handling desert heat without water, while in combat for over three hours.

Back in the wire now, 10th Mountain broke off and rolled to their lakeside hootches; we rolled, alone and quiet, back to the Scouts' hootch. Pulling up outside, I said to Martin, "Now I know how those boys felt in Mogadishu," reflecting on being without water, under heavy fire, and missing essential equipment, such as spotter scopes, extra mags, and extra water—all the pre-mission checks you usually do before you go out.

Getting out of the Humvee, we were all so tired that we barely spoke. All the Scouts ran out to greet us.

"I got me a good confirmed kill," I said to Sergeant John Howerton from San Antonio, Texas. He nodded and smiled—which knocked me out, because he very rarely smiled—saying, "We were all listening on the radio. We heard it." I thanked him and chugged down a canteen of cool water. It was the best water I've ever had in my life, and after drinking it, I got my second wind. I took my Kevlar helmet off and noticed that a white ring of salt covered my helmet, vest, and blouse. Seeing all that salt over my gear and uniform, I shrugged to myself and said, "Damn, it was hot out there." I kept drinking water and stripped my weapon, cleaned it, and did a round count. I pulled out the three empty brass from my pocket and set them in the black case for the SR-25. I made sure that our Scouts and snipers understood that now, in early October 2003, the enemy was digging in IEDs right in the roads and then repaving the roads with fresh asphalt (or dirt, if it was a dirt road).

Having cleaned my weapon, I began rethinking my actions in the firefight. The main criticism I directed at myself was, *Maybe next time I'll bring a little bit of water. And either my spotter or RTO, and a spotting scope*. I was too tired to go to chow. I ate a few snacks that I'd left on my cot, stuff from care packages. Cooling down, I assembled my SR-25 and wiped the glass with a soft cotton cloth, on each end of the scope. Martin came by and we headed over to talk with Lieutenant Swartwood and Lopez. Briefly, we went over the firefight—not with the detail of say, an after-action report, but with enough information to give them essential intelligence about the insurgents.

We Scouts liked to call Lopez "The Neck," for his neck's strange ability to grow in the grueling Western Iraqi desert. This was mysterious, as our own necks shrank from the desert heat. Whenever he'd eat cookies and drink coffee, we'd say, "He's feeding the neck; the neck is growing again!" Arroyo did the best impression of The Neck. Every time Lopez would call out, "Who's going to chow?" Arroyo would always sound off in the back of his throat like a pig squealing, as if it were feeding time at the trough. His impression was flawless and we'd all fall out laughing. I'm sure Lopez heard Arroyo do that more than once, but probably thought we were just laughing at each other.

By now it was nighttime, and I walked over to Robi's hootch to check on him. He was kicking back on his cot with his headphones on, listening to '50s doo-wop. He slipped his headphones down as I walked in and said, "What's up, Sergeant?"

"You good?" I asked, and he nodded, saying, "Yeah, I'm good."

"You did good out there today," I replied. I gave him a thumbs-up as I walked out, saying, "Make sure you get some chow tonight."

"All right, Sergeant," he said in his usual even tone. Robi was always polite and easygoing. He'd been orphaned as a young boy and was adopted by a Mormon family in Utah.

As I walked out of the hootch, Martin joined me and asked if I wanted to go to chow with him. He told me that the after-action report with 10th Mountain would be in the morning. (As with all missions, an AAR came either right after the mission or the next morning, depending on the commander's call.)

"Well, I'm gonna stick here and wait for the show," I said, checking my watch. It was 18:45 (6:45 p.m.): time for the nightly enemy mortar barrage. Kicking back outside my hootch, I thought back on the day as the mortars came, a fifteen-minute barrage, thudding all over our base. They sounded heavy and loud, like 81mm or 82mm mortars. I knew this wasn't enough to interrupt Lopez's chow; he needed to feed The Neck, and coffee and cookies alone wouldn't do the job. Mortars be damned, The Neck must expand!

Truly exhausted, and damn glad that we'd all made it back in the wire alive, I crashed at about nine that evening, until it was my turn for guard rotation on the wall near our Scouts' hootch. After guard duty, I went back to sleep.

The sun was just breaking over the eastern horizon, coming up slowly over the desert, when I gathered Martin and Robi the next day. We told Lopez, "We're going to chow and then on to the AAR," and he said, "Okay." After chow, we got to Captain Kirkpatrick's hootch to link up with 10th Mountain for the AAR. The captain came right up to me and said, "Heard you made one helluva shot."

"Thanks to Martin, absolutely, sir," I said as he reached out a hand. We shook hands and he smiled and nodded at me.

The AAR went swiftly. We all agreed that the firefight the day before had proven that in any situation, even a leaders' recon, combat can go south quickly. Any situation in war, however calm it may seem at the outset, can deteriorate at the drop of a hat. The flip side, of course, is that in war, how you react to such a rapidly deteriorating situation will have a helluva lot to do with the outcome. We hadn't hesitated to take the fight to the enemy once we'd been engaged, and that had a great deal to do with our survival; our will to live and prevail in that action is what ultimately saved us.

Captain Kirkpatrick ended the AAR by saying, "With what happened, great job on everybody's part." It was clear that he had no qualms or issues with our actions in the firefight. We all nodded to him and walked out. I remember thinking, as we left the AAR, that due to our actions in the firefight, 10th Mountain could now rely on us and would no doubt call on us again. I knew that they were happy with us. Once you've earned someone's trust and respect in combat, it's a bond that's hard to break.

I later learned from Mike Tucker that Captain Kirkpatrick had talked to him about me in late November 2003, saying, "LeBleu is very solid in combat, trustworthy and reliable. He's a real shit-hot sniper and I'm lucky to have him with my men, on missions." That was mighty kind of Captain Kirkpatrick. I remember thinking in early October 2003 that 10th Mountain was my family now; it seemed that everywhere 10th Mountain went, I went with them. I learned to think like them and to anticipate their moves; I was with them so often, I could read their body language on missions and know what their next step would be.

At one point in October, I said to Lopez, "I might as well just hootch with them." It was late in the evening and he was eating cookies and drinking coffee (feeding The Neck!). He was happy that evening, with his snacks, the mysterious neck growing again, and he nodded toward me and grunted, "We'll just fuckin' transfer you over to 10th Mountain!"

Declining his generous offer, a true sign of charity on his part, I walked away, laughing, with Arroyo's imitation of Lopez ringing in my head. What the hell; we had to get our kicks somehow. Comedy was the only thing that kept us sane at war in Iraq. If we weren't making scorpions and camel spiders fight each other in the sand, then we were poking fun at each other, like two brothers living in the same house. In the end, boys will be boys. To paraphrase the great Brooklyn Dodgers catcher, Roy Campanella, every man should keep a bit of the little boy in him, to keep him happy and keep him humble.

All in all, Lopez was a good platoon sergeant. Even though we poked fun at him, he was always working behind-the-scene deals to get us more comfortable living situations, and, of course, trying to get us better food. We all appreciated what he did for the platoon.

With the AAR done, Robi drove me and Martin back to our Scouts' hootch. I continued on daylight missions with 10th Mountain and going over the wall on night reconnaissance, as usual.

We searched for any kind of field intelligence that we could get on "The Mad Mortarman," who was hitting us like clockwork every night, between 6:30 and 7:30 p.m.

After a week, Lopez informed me that I would be attached to the 504th at Forward Operating Base St. Mere, because their Scout platoon needed another school-qualified sniper. At the time, they only had one sniper in 504th Scouts who had graduated from U.S. Army Sniper School.

Upon my arrival to my new home for the next month, I could immediately see how vast and huge and dusty St. Mere was; it was so big that Delta Force commandos and other U.S. Army Special Forces stationed there had an entire sub-compound all to themselves, located in a secluded, fairly heavily wooded corner of the massive base.

We rolled up to the 504th Scouts' hootch, the dust choking us. When Lopez dropped me off, he introduced me to their Scouts' platoon sergeant and platoon leader. Lopez had asked me to leave the SR-25 with 505th Scouts, so that McGuire and the other NCOs could get some good hands-on experience with it. I carried with me to St. Mere my M24 7.62x51mm sniper rifle, along with my sidearm. Specialist Jason Bailor, a young, very quiet Scout from Tennessee, had come with me as my new spotter. Bailor carried his M4 with a silencer. He was about five-foot-ten, slim and very self-contained.

We were switching guys around in the different teams, to ensure that our Scouts were all cross-trained on all of our weapons—M24, .50 cal Barrett sniper rifle, SR-25, M4/M203 grenade launcher, M4 assault rifle, and 9mm Beretta sidearm. Myself and fellow sniper team leaders, Staff Sergeant David MacGillivary and Sergeant John Howerton, had also spent a lot of time, when not on missions, in training the 505th Scouts on firing the "Ma Deuce" and the MK19 40mm mounted grenade launcher. Howerton was always on the case, giving classes and ensuring that everyone knew what the hell they were doing. I always tip my hat to him for that.

Arroyo was with me, along with Bailor, filling out my team as the RTO. Arroyo carried his M4/M203 and his field radio. Before rolling back to Volturno, Lopez handed Arroyo a bag of Oreo cookies, grinning and saying, "Chow down, you little fuckers!" It was all Arroyo could do to keep from falling over, laughing; his face beet-red, he choked out, "Roger that, Sergeant!" As Lopez drove away, Arroyo came up to me and said, "Sergeant LeBleu, look what The Neck gave us!", and he made his hilarious imitation of Lopez—even Bailor, who was hard to get a laugh out of, busted up laughing.

A 504th Scout sergeant came over and welcomed us, guiding us over to some empty hootches. He introduced us to his fellow Scouts in the 504th. Not all of their Scouts were so welcoming; there was a bit of tension in the air. I looked around and noticed a black flag hanging on the wall above their cots. It read DON'T TREAD ON ME. It was your typical patriotic grunts' hootch, with many voluptuous women in their birthday suits also featured on the walls. I broke the ice by saying, "I guess we're your bastard stepbrothers for a while." They relaxed now, grinning and nodding at me. It never hurts to poke a little fun at yourself in combat to help put others at ease. Ain't that the truth! When people around you know that you're comfortable in your own skin, it makes them more comfortable to be with you in combat, and generally speaking, takes their minds off the hardships of war.

Once we'd set up on our new cots and got mission-oriented—with all of our gear ready to go on a mission, at a moment's notice—I told my team, "Might as well get comfortable, because we're going to be here for a while." Bailor and Arroyo nodded. I remember saying to Arroyo, "And no, Arroyo, you *can't* hang up your gang colors!" He smirked and said, "That's fucked up, Sergeant." I always teased Arroyo about being a gangbanger from East LA, even though he was very much a straight-arrow kid and had an honorable relationship with his family. They really cared about him and he very much cared about them. All in all, I was glad to have him on my team.

That evening, after we'd set up our quarters in the small concrete hootch, the cots lined up side by side, I grabbed my team. The sun was just starting to settle in the west, and I said, "Let's take a walk." I wanted to get a feel for our immediate surroundings. We checked out an outdoor weight room that had a desert camouflage net hanging over it, near our hootch. I nodded toward it and told Bailor and Arroyo, "When we're not on missions, we'll be spending our time here. If I'm gonna have morons on my team, at least they'll be strong morons!"

Of course, Arroyo grinned and replied, "That's fucked up, Sergeant." No question—this was his favorite saying when in my presence. Bailor, quiet as usual, just grinned and spit out some tobacco juice. He always had dip or tobacco chew in his mouth, except when he was sleeping. I remember it always annoyed the hell out of me, even back in my earlier duty as a Ranger, seeing soldiers spit everywhere in cups and in their sinks. Maybe it was just because I didn't chew, but either way, it's a nasty habit.

Every night we went on reconnaissance missions, and our specific mission was night reconnaissance on the Cloverleaf. Each night we'd rotate to a different corner of the Cloverleaf, on reconnaissance for insurgents laying IEDs on or underneath the overpass. Our rules of engagement were quite simple: If it looked out of place, it *was* out of place. For instance, if a vehicle pulled over to the side of the road for more than two minutes, it became a threat, especially if they opened their hood or trunk. The international sign of suspicious activity, with any vehicle, is if it is pulled over for no apparent reason. If no one is coming out of the vehicle and taking a piss, the radiator is not steaming, the tires are not flat, and it's clear that there are no obvious mechanical problems, then that vehicle is definitely dirty.

Obviously, if someone in the vehicle was carrying a weapon, or if they were digging, then we had full authority to kill them, under our rules of engagement. One thing to keep in mind, vital to any combat, is that a sniper's rules of engagement are always different than regular infantry, in any war.

Of that month of counter-IED reconnaissance missions on the Cloverleaf, there is one mission in particular that stands out in my memory. I will never forget it. It still bothers me to this day that I was denied a chance to kill three insurgents at close range and prevent them from laying an IED.

I felt that what happened that night marked the turning point, the moment when our leadership—beginning with our commander in chief and going all the way down to battalion-level command in Iraq—started giving away the initiative to insurgents and terrorists in Iraq. There is no excuse for this. Even blind men can see what a disaster the Iraq War has become since 2003, and I feel that the U.S. failure to strike and kill insurgents and terrorists in Iraq has contributed to our failure. Bush shifted the goalposts in Iraq in May 2003, before the U.S. and the Coalition had ever crossed the goal line in the first place.

Once you've sent combat troops downrange, you can't win at a press conference what you haven't first won on a battlefield. Bush has proven by his failure of command in the Iraq War that one Seeing Eye dog is not enough for him—he rates two Seeing Eye dogs, at least.

I remember that particular night of Cloverleaf reconnaissance like it was yesterday. Like most nights, it was steaming hot, with the smells of sewage and tire fires and diesel even more intense at night. Bailor was my spotter and Arroyo, my radioman. Walking to our hide, which was actually on the southwest corner of the Cloverleaf, not far from Volturno, we patrolled slowly around, looking for any fresh insurgent footprints, jeep tracks, or motorcycle tracks in the sand.

We came up to an oversized rock, took a knee, and conducted SLLS: Stop, Look, Listen, and Smell. This is a well-known tactic used on patrols. While conducting SLLS, which usually lasts about fifteen to twenty minutes, out of nowhere I heard Arabic voices behind me, to my south. Automatically, I thought, *This could be the spotter for the Mad Mortarman*, the one behind the mortar and rocket attacks on Volturno every night. I gave hand signals to Bailor and Arroyo to be silent, and pointed south. I gave signals to

Arroyo to cover the desert north, and pull security for us, while Bailor and I slowly low-crawled toward the voices.

We'd gone about 50 meters and soon came upon a 15-foot depression, big enough to hold four black Mercedes-Benzes, with five insurgents all standing outside around the cars. I was checking them out with my naked eye, not using a scope at that moment. Two men were smoking cigarettes and one man was on a cell phone, staring toward Volturno. I marked the man on the cell phone as the mortar spotter, for what would turn out to be mortar attacks on Volturno that night. I slowly pushed back from the edge of the depression, dust and sand all gritty on my neck and seeping into my blouse. In complete silence, I gave hand signals to Bailor on how many enemy there were. I could clearly see that the insurgents were all carrying AK-47 Kalashnikov assault rifles.

I gave Bailor all the field Intel on the enemy through hand and arm signals, maintaining stealth, and gave him a thumbs-up when I finished to ensure that he understood me. He nodded quickly back at me. Turning slowly, I looked back at Arroyo, giving him the hand signal to call in the field Intel: "Five insurgents, small arms, possible mortar spotter on cell phone."

Arroyo then gave me the thumbs-up, indicating he'd made the call to Task Force 1Panther on Volturno. Once I saw his thumbs-up, I was not going to wait around for their response, so I low-crawled back to the edge of the crater. As we raised our rifles to our shoulders, scoping the enemy, I zeroed in on the mortar spotter, still on his cell phone. Bailor zeroed in on the closest guy carrying a Kalashnikov. I remember thinking, *This has to go down fast*, because there were five of them and three of us.

As I set my M24 live, taking it off safe, and began to squeeze the trigger, Arroyo came halfway over to me and said softly, "Sergeant, stand by." I took my finger off the trigger, aggravated. Arroyo informed me in a very low voice that the platoon leader of 504th Scouts, in radio transmissions with Task Force 1Panther, had ordered us to stand down because 1Panther was going to fire on the enemy's grid location with mortars.

It took every ounce of energy in me not to kill the enemy. We had perfect line of sight on them. We were so close, I could hear the insurgent mortar spotter talking in guttural, rapid-fire Arabic on his cell phone. I could see the ash dropping from the insurgents' cigarettes as they ambled around, glaring toward Volturno, their Kalashnikovs all loaded with one magazine each, their rifles at the low ready, held at the waist. I continued staring Arroyo in the eye, meanwhile, and said, "Are you fuckin' serious? How are they going to shoot mortars at these insurgents if no one has given them the grid?"

"I don't know, Sergeant, that's just what they said. It's pretty fucked up, isn't it?" Arroyo said, his voice still low in the night.

I gritted my teeth and asked him, "How long until they fire?"

"Two mikes," he replied, meaning two minutes.

Looking at Arroyo, I realized I had to get him and Bailor the hell out of there, without being seen by the enemy in the open desert. What both Task Force 1Panther and the 504th platoon leader had failed to understand, at that moment, is that my sniper team was still in the kill zone for the planned mortar attack on the insurgents. We had to move immediately, quick smart. We low-crawled backwards far enough so that we wouldn't be spotted, rose up, and ran hunched over, sprinting, knowing we had to get at least 300 meters away. I kept pushing Arroyo and Bailor to hustle it up, and finally, thank God, we came upon a boulder. We settled down behind it, in the prone.

I kept my eyes on a dirt road leading west out of the crater, keeping my scope on it, saying to myself, *If Task Force 1Panther doesn't kill these bastards with mortars, I'll kill them myself.* Within seconds, I could hear mortar tubes launch from Volturno, with the first round falling very short, on the eastern side of the crater, rocks and sand and debris spraying everywhere. I couldn't see a thing at that moment, as we were all covered with dirt and rocks. I laid down my rifle and yelled to Bailor and Arroyo, "Hold on boys, this is gonna be loud!"

We all covered our ears, laying in the prone, waiting for the next 81mm mortar rounds to hit. I kept glancing up, in spurts, to see where the rounds were hitting as they continued to slam into the sand. After five minutes of mortar barrage, the paratroopers stopped firing; there was so much dust, none of my team could see the crater now. We sat there for a few minutes, waiting for the dust to settle.

Once the dust had dissipated, I said to Arroyo, "Pull security; me and Bailor are moving up." He nodded.

We patrolled quickly up to the edge of the crater, our rifles shouldered, ready to fire. As we came up to the crater, we saw two dead bodies. One of the Mercedes was blown up. Somehow, in all of that mortar fire, the other three insurgents had gotten away. I remember thinking that the first short rounds were the window the insurgents used to escape. It doesn't take long to turn a key in the ignition—especially if the key is already in and that vehicle is ready to roll—and slam on the gas and get out of Dodge, anywhere in the world. This whole situation was a classic example of someone with a radio in their hand instead of a rifle, denying a warrior with a rifle in his hand a key opportunity to kill the enemy. To paraphrase Patton: There are no second chances in war; you get one chance to kill the enemy, and you won't get it twice.

Although I was nearly suffocating with anger and disappointment, I understood the choice between saving the lives of my team, now, or killing the enemy. I chose my men. I knew for a fact that there were plenty more insurgents down the road. I turned to Bailor and said in a low voice, "Let's go." We ran back to Arroyo and took a knee, telling him, "We will not make that same mistake again." Kneeling in the sand, I asked Arroyo and Bailor, "Are you good?" They replied, "Roger," and we moved out, heading north through the scrub brush and sand and rocky terrain to our hide site in the desert. We planned to be there all night.

It was probably just thirty minutes later, with the night very quiet now, that a semitrailer came off of Highway 1, the north-south highway in Fallujah, and stopped about 400 meters away from us. At first, I paid it no mind, giving it the two-minute rule. I whispered to Bailor, "You got that semi?"

"Yeah, I got it," he said, scoping it with his night observation device (NOD), eyeballing the truck.

Laying there, watching the truck, I noted that five minutes had already gone by. I confirmed with Bailor that the semi had been there for five minutes. My gut told me to get closer and check it out. Right before I told my team to get ready to move closer, at that very second, three men came out of the passenger's side of the semi and stood in one spot for three minutes. At that time, they had nothing in their hands. It seemed to me that they were testing the waters.

I told Bailor and Arroyo, "Be still; don't move. We've got three guys out on the passenger's side of that semi." For the next three minutes, we watched them intently. One insurgent then went to the cab of the semi and pulled out a shovel.

I whispered to Bailor and Arroyo, "This should be interesting."

Arroyo replied, grinning, "Maybe he has to take a shit and he wants to bury it."

Bailor and I turned to Arroyo and just shook our heads, grinning; we both wanted to laugh so hard but we had to maintain noise discipline.

After what had just happened, with the 504th platoon leader denying my team the kill on five insurgents, I was skeptical about Arroyo calling my field intelligence on the IED diggers, but I knew it was standard operating procedure. Arroyo got right on the horn. The man with the shovel was digging very fast and very intensely on the shoulder of the road, on the passenger's side of the semi.

*If I ever need some yard work done, this is the guy to call*, I reckoned, because of his ability to dig so hard and so quick.

But I knew he wasn't there looking for buried treasure. I could make out the two other guys, pulling security for him; I couldn't make out if they had weapons. I wanted to get closer and confirm whether or not they had any weapons before I shot them, however. So I ordered my team to pick up and move 200 meters, which is actually unorthodox in the sniper community, and is certainly not recommended.

I was trusting my gut. I've always been a fan of getting close and knowing my enemy before we danced. Even in Sniper School, I would always get closer than the instructors recommended. Some people called it ballsy and even a little reckless, but I call it knowing your job. And as Major Robert Rogers, the great commander of Rogers's Rangers in the French and Indian Wars, said, "In boldness lies safety." What is bold and daring is often the absolute effective action, in war, but to those who were not in line when God was handing out guile and audacity, being bold and daring in battle will always look a bit reckless. Was it reckless for Rogers to lead two hundred Rangers 400 miles behind enemy lines, in 1759? To the armchair soldier or civilian in the U.S. Department of Defense, no doubt that still sounds pretty irresponsible. But to those who are Rangers in our time, Rogers's classic deep reconnaissance and raid of the St. Francis's Abenaki Camp in Canada in 1759 was not only bold, it was also incredibly clever and born of masterful guile.

Hustling up, we covered the 200 meters to the semi quickly, sneaking up behind them and getting on our bellies in the sand. I raised my sniper rifle, looking through my PVS10 night-vision scope, and was surprised by how much I could see. I could make out the sweat on their backs and count their eyelashes. I could tell now that the men had no weapons, and that the digger was well into his job—clearly, digging a hole for an IED. The two lookouts kept glancing in all directions and talking in Arabic. We were so close, we could hear their conversations. The lookout closest to the digger kept saying in Arabic, "Faster, faster, dig faster."

I looked at Arroyo and he was already on the horn, whispering on the radio what was going down right in front of us. Being that this was a prime IED magnet, and the key Coalition supply route in Fallujah, it was clear that this was an IED in the making. I remember thinking, *This is a prime opportunity to gain field intelligence on how the insurgents place IEDs.* Once I'd gathered that intelligence to my satisfaction, I whispered to Bailor, "Get ready to take out the lookout facing south."

He nodded. Finding myself in the same situation that I'd been in an hour ago, again Arroyo came back with, "Stand down, Sergeant." I replied, "Negative. Tell Command that the insurgents are placing an IED, which is well within ROE that was briefed to us. We can't afford to lose more friendlies because of IEDs."

Arroyo relayed my message to Task Force 1Panther.

Now I grabbed the radio from Arroyo as the 504th platoon leader got on the horn. He told me, "I understand, but this is coming from Volturno."

"Stand by," I replied quickly.

As I switched frequencies to Volturno, I told Arroyo and Bailor, "I can't believe this shit is happening again, twice in one night." I connected with Volturno, saying, "This is Hawk3. I have three insurgents placing an IED at the Cloverleaf, as we speak. Permission to fire. Over." I repeated the transmission, to make it absolutely clear, saying, "This is Hawk3, I say again. I have three insurgents placing an IED at the Cloverleaf, as we speak. Permission to fire, how copy, over?"

Volturno replied, in a my-way-or-the-highway tone: "Negative. You will not fire. You will get a grid for the IED. How copy?"

I knew I was talking to an officer from Task Force 1Panther who was probably the battalion radio watch officer that night, who had no clue as to what was going on.

"Be advised. We cannot afford to lose more friendlies," I replied.

The IED digger had stopped and was now placing the IED, a box-shaped crate with wires hanging from all sides—wired and set to blow. I could see detonation cord, called "det cord" by demolitions specialists, wrapped around the IED.

"Negative," he replied. "You will not fire. You will get a grid for the IED location. Do you understand, Hawk3?"

The IED was now in place and the digger was furiously shoveling dirt and sand over it, making sure it was buried and ready to kill American soldiers.

"I understand that you're making a mistake," I replied to the great, all-knowing officer who had just ensured that more Americans would be killed by IEDs in Iraq. I tossed the phone away and Arroyo grabbed the handset.

Looking at Bailor, I said, "Do me a favor and go run up and pat that guy on the back, since we can't kill him for laying an IED."

I got the grid for the location of the IED and gave it to Arroyo, who got on the horn back to the 504th platoon leader and relayed the grid.

I felt like I'd been let down and lied to. Right at that moment, I started questioning what people's motives were to fight and win this war. We were all very dejected and downhearted as we watched the insurgents place an IED right in front of us. We knew that our own command had denied us a prime opportunity to kill a total of eight insurgents that night, and nothing justified their gutless actions.

We had no choice but to watch the three insurgents finish placing the IED, watching as the digger shoveled the last of the dirt over the device, tamping it down with his feet, and leveling off the dirt on the shoulder of the road. I felt like we were being forced to watch one of our comrades being beheaded in an insurgent snuff video, right in front of us.

Their work completed, the digger threw his shovel in the semi and joined his two fellow insurgents in the cab, the engine racing now. They zoomed away in the night, disappearing beyond an overpass south along the highway. Once they had left, I looked at Bailor and Arroyo and said, "There's no need for us to be here anymore. Let's push back to our original hide site."

Moving silently and slowly in the desert night, we set up back in our original hide site. The rest of the night went by uneasily; none of us spoke. I could feel the morale sucked out of us, as if our command was a morale vampire. The fighting spirit was being zapped out of us by our leadership's ridiculous decision to stop us from killing eight insurgents, and to leave an IED, buried and wired and set to kill Americans, in the side of the key Coalition supply route for all of Western Iraq.

Lying in the hide site, I could see the disgust and disappointment on my team's faces. I knew I had to break their train of thought and get them back in the fight, because we were still at war, on a mission, and we had no time to feel sorry for ourselves.

"Despite everything that happened tonight, keep your mind in the game," I said. "Because this is when you get hurt—when you lose focus, when you lose morale. There will be plenty of time later to bitch and moan about what went down tonight. But we still have a job to do," I said to them, knowing that we could not afford any lack of professionalism or failure of discipline.

"Yeah, but it's so fucked up, Sergeant. They should've let us do our job," Bailor replied, the frustration in his voice all too evident.

"What's wrong, Bailor? You don't like fattening up all of Command's résumé, especially our president's? You don't like making sure that we're buying yachts for congressmen?"

"Yeah, no shit, Sergeant," Bailor replied, Arroyo grunting his agreement, "That's right."

As always, my attempt at comedy in combat had the right effect on Bailor and Arroyo. They began to relax, and I could see that their heads were back in the game—they were back in the fight again, where I wanted—and needed—them to be.

After a long night on reconnaissance, I could see the sun coming up on the eastern horizon. The everyday scents of Western Iraq—sewage, burning tires, diesel, and the pleasant smell of fresh baked bread—were all around us. "Let's move," I told Bailor and Arroyo, and we moved to our exfil grid—the map point we'd plotted before the mission, where we would be picked up by 504th Scouts. Everyone was a little tired—from being up all night, and from the frustration and aggravation we'd experienced.

We waited behind a dirt mound in the prone, at our exfil point. I heard a Humvee nearing our position and I told my team to get ready. We held our rifles at the ready, all of us taking a knee and scanning the desert in all the points of the compass. I could see the driver of the Humvee now and waved low and to one side as he rolled up toward us. We jumped on board, leaping on the back as it came to a rolling stop, and I latched the tow strap and hollered, "We're good!" We rolled off, back toward St. Mere, passing Volturno. I cringed, glancing at Volturno, thinking of the night before and their command's refusal to order us to kill the insurgents.

Even though we were coming up toward the safe zone, toward the somewhat-comfortable home we had at St. Mere, I said to my team, "Keep pulling security—we're not home yet." I wanted to make sure they were on the same page as me. We were still outside the wire, and we had to stay 110 percent hard and sharp and smart. I could feel the heat rising as we came back in the wire. Dust caked us from the long night and the ride back to St. Mere. We got off the back of the Humvee slowly, grabbed our gear and rifles, and headed to our hootch.

As we were setting our gear down, I said to Bailor and Arroyo, looking at our cots, "Well, this is the only thing that has made sense all night." Wiped out, they just smiled as they set their rifles and rounds and gear down. "Once you set your gear down, come outside for a minute," I said, and they nodded. The sun was very strong outside. Being out all night, our night vision had not left us yet and we were squinting; the sun was nearly blinding us. As we walked over to the side of the hootch, I pulled them in closely and said in a low voice, "We all know what happened last night was fucked up. But I don't need you running your mouth about it. It's my fight, so I'll fight it. I want us to maintain the professionalism we came here with."

Their eyes hard, they both said, "Roger." I knew that they wanted to voice their opinions, but given the respect and trust I'd earned from them, I was pretty sure that they would let me handle it.

"Go get some sleep," I said, nodding toward our hootch.

After they crashed, I poked my head inside the 504th Scouts' hootch, saying to the platoon sergeant, "Hey, Sergeant, can you come outside for a second?"

Waiting outside, I was thinking, *Everybody must know what's going on. Either folks heard it on the radio, or they can see the tension from my team.*

The 504th Scouts platoon sergeant was about six foot even, lean, broad-shouldered, with reddish-blond hair. I nodded to him, and before I could even say anything, he walked over to me and said, "I know last night was fucked up. But it wasn't our call. We were in Volturno's sector. You should have just shot the mother-fuckers. Next time, just shoot."

"Roger that, Sergeant, but we don't want to be stepping on any-one's toes," I replied, folding my arms and smiling. We were on good terms, and he replied, "We can't step on toes if we don't see them," reinforcing his earlier advice to shoot first next time with-out calling the situation in on the horn. As he walked away, I said to him, "I don't think everyone understands the ROE put out, so maybe you could help me reiterate that to everyone," thinking of their platoon leader's hands being tied due to the ongoing "sector battles" between St. Mere and Volturno. "And by the way," I added, "here's the grid for the IED we saw dug and placed last night."

"Yeah, I'm working on that," he replied, nodding to me.

I could understand, somewhat, why the platoon leader had countermanded my decision to fire on the five insurgents and their black Mercedes-Benzes the night before. He was pretty much stuck in the middle of a bad situation, one not of his own making. Looking back, this was indeed the start of many such battles that took place between the 504th and the 505th; it was very unfortunate, because the commanders' pride and the inter-army turf wars seemed to be more important than killing the enemy and winning the war.

I knew in the back of my mind that this was the beginning of a different kind of war. I could see clearly that our leadership, both civilian and military, was failing to understand what it really takes to win a war. And failing to read our own history, as Americans at war.

Victory in war involves getting a little dirty with the business end of a rifle, the cutting edge of a fighting knife, and the pin of a grenade. When the Marines won at Tarawa and Okinawa and Iwo Jima in WWII, they did not hesitate to tape grenades around sticks of dynamite, wire the grenade pins together, and then pull the pins all at one time, throwing the improvised bomb into Japanese caves and bunkers. A Marine on a flamethrower would follow. Marines throwing grenades and firing shotguns, Thompson submachine guns, and machine guns would follow the flamethrowers. And no one denied those Marines the chance to strike and kill their enemy. Americans, in our time, have forgotten just what it took for the Greatest Generation to win at war. And war never changes.

I knew I wasn't the only one to be denied the opportunity to kill the enemy. Ever since the war turned Politically Correct, denials were becoming a trend. They were a dime a dozen, unfortunately. I guess this is where careers became more important than our freedom and protecting our country. I have seen numerous articles written by enlisted and veterans alike, complaining about how they can't do their jobs anymore, because the higher-ups are more interested in their résumés.

Stressed out from the night, and in no mood for chow, I stretched out on my cot and got a few hours of sleep. I'd decided that we'd clean our weapons after some much-needed rest. I knew that we'd be going out on another mission that night, as we did every night throughout the rest of October, attached to the 504th Scouts. We slept for five hours and got some chow, came back and cleaned our weapons, and then prepared our gear and rifles for that night's mission on the Cloverleaf.

The platoon sergeant walked in when I was sitting on my cot, cleaning my weapon. "I guess that grid checks out," he said. "There was an IED there. We called Explosive Ordnance Disposal and gave them the grid. EOD disarmed it and dug it out," he said.

"How 'bout that," I said. Thanks to my team, we'd saved some lives that day. It still made my blood boil, however, knowing that the IED cell—the insurgents who'd dug and placed the roadside bomb—were still free and clear to kill my comrades because I hadn't been given the authority to kill them the night before. Who knows how many IEDs they went on to place in Fallujah and Western Iraq, and God only knows how many Americans that IED cell went on to kill.

We needed Patton, and we had no Patton. And we needed a president and commander in chief with the resolve and will and tenacity of FDR. Instead, we had Bush, who knows as much about fighting and winning wars as Dick Cheney knows about firearms safety.

After a month of reconnaissance and counter-IED missions with the 504th Scouts, I got word that my team was going to be picked up and transferred back to 505th Scouts, where The Neck ruled with grace and good humor. Our whole platoon had gotten word that we were transferring up to a known radiation site and bomb factory, called the "Rad Site." We packed all our gear, weapons, and ammunition on a convoy of Humvees and rolled about five hours southwest, far from the western bank of the Euphrates, in the general direction of Jordan.

We were the only unit from Task Force 1Panther on the western shores of the Euphrates River. There were trash-can–sized IED holes all along the roads leading to our new base, from which Coalition counter-IED teams had pulled roadside bombs on both sides of the broken, worn-down asphalt road leading to 1st Armored Division's supply base. The massive supply base for 1st AD was an hour east of the Rad Site, while 1st AD was fighting in Baghdad, eight hours away by truck or Humvee.

We were deep in the desert now, all by our lonesome. Rolling inside the Rad Site in early November, a paratrooper greeted us from behind a .50 caliber heavy machine gun, pulling security on the front gate. About 25 meters inside the gate, we stopped at a ramshackle concrete hut.

Inside, the walls and floors were covered in human feces. Lopez told us, "This is it; this is our new home." Everyone looked at each other, in shock, as if to say, "You have *got* to be kidding!" The stench from the human waste was so overwhelming, we had to put bandanas and rags around our noses and mouths. Some of us had *khaffiyehs*, so we wrapped them around our faces to repel the stench. Staring at the building, I said, "Well, I want to make a complaint to the Homeowners' Association!"

Everyone busted up laughing, and I turned to Arroyo. "Hell, you should be used to this! Isn't this how your house is, back in LA?"

He grinned, laughing, and said, "That's fucked up, Sergeant!"

"No, what's fucked up is us having to clean Iraqi shit off the walls."

Through the stench, you could smell a strange, cherry-like scent in the air; we were later told that was the sweet aroma of cobalt radiation. Under Saddam, the Rad Site had been an artillery factory and a nuclear processing site. Surrounding our great new home, which exemplified hygienic standards of the highest quality in Western Iraq, were oversized bomb and artillery shell warehouses, which also held T-54 tanks, T-72 tanks, and 90mm and 105mm artillery cannons. Clothes were scattered everywhere. You could tell that everyone in the factory had left in a hurry. I came to discover that nighttime at the Rad Site was very spooky. I'd walk around the ruins of the artillery factory in the evening, and late at night, looking out at the desert in all directions.

On that first day, however, we had to get like Mr. Clean and sanitize the hell out of our new hootch. Lopez said, "Clean the fuckin' hootch, you fuckers!" He went over to the paratroopers and got some cleaning supplies: brooms, mops, Brillo pads, Simple Green detergent, Pine-Sol, and sponges. We all took deep breaths and took off our blouses. All the privates and specialists soaked the walls and floors with water, which increased the god-awful stench, and the intense heat from the desert sun only added to the grotesque fecal aroma. We were, literally, now standing in a sea of shit, giving new meaning to the phrase, "Life is a sea of shit; you can either sink, swim, or go in boats."

But hope arrived in the furious scrubbing of our Scouts, who tossed gallons of Simple Green and Pine-Sol all over the floors and walls.

"I want this place cleaner than Gibson's ass!" I said, referring to Private First Class Gibson from Colorado, who did not understand the fundamentals of hygiene. The platoon broke up laughing, and Arroyo said, "Damn, I don't know if we can get it that clean, Sergeant!"

The rest of us moved furniture outside to air it out and clean it; luckily, there was no shit on the furniture, so the desert heat and strong winds removed the smell as our Scouts finished cleaning the hootch. We set up our cots once the hootch was dry, each team taking a separate room. Lopez wanted everything in easy reach, so we hung all our gear from nails hammered into the plaster and concrete walls. Rather than using the Iraqi bathroom, which was a hole in the ground, we installed piss tubes made of regular black PVC pipes in the dirt, about 30 meters across from the Scouts' hootch.

Before nightfall, we set up our communications on top of the roof, piecing together our antennas and wires so we could communicate with Task Force 1Panther and all nearby Coalition units, such as the 1st AD supply base. There was a good scent now of pine and alcohol in the air; the stench of fecal matter had gone with the wind.

We sniper team leaders—Sergeant John Howerton, Staff Sergeant David MacGillivary, Staff Sergeant Jason Martin, Sergeant Patrick McGuire, and myself—set up radio watches. Basically, for our entire time at the Rad Site, whoever was not out on a desert recon-naissance mission stayed on radio watch at our Scouts' hootch.

That night, we all walked around together, checking out the base, clearing small huts and buildings, making sure the base was secure. No one had given us a heads-up on the large abandoned base, and we had no field intelligence on nearby insurgent activ-ity. Walking around, we assessed the walls for possible breach points, where insurgents could cross over into the base and attack us. We noticed the four guard towers at each corner of the base, lined with sandbags.

Back at our hootch, Lopez met us with intelligence on upcom-ing missions in the desert. Our desert reconnaissance missions and sniper missions in November 2003 were geared directly toward capturing or killing Saddam Hussein. There was some intelligence that he was moving in a ten- to fifteen-vehicle convoy made up of black Mercedes-Benzes and black SUVs, moving on back roads throughout Western Iraq between Jordan and Mosul. We were also told that there had been a lot of recent insurgent activity in the sec-tor west of the Euphrates.

With our new home established and the scent of Pine-Sol pleasantly thick in the dry desert air, Lopez said, "We're probably only going to be out here two to three weeks." We all looked at each other, realizing we'd likely be back at Volturno before Thanksgiv-ing. Little did we know, within a week, all of our gear would be dropped off, and our orders changed to *We don't know when you're coming back to Volturno.*

We started missions immediately. As night drew close, my team, Howerton's team, and MacGillivary's team prepped gear for our first night's reconnaissance of the desert near the Rad Site. On this terrain, deep in the desert west of the Euphrates, we had to rely purely on stealth, because there was nothing in all directions for at least three miles. As we waited for the sun to drop and night to take command, we coordinated with all the watchtowers—especially the two front towers—letting them know that we were going out the wire on foot that night.

We ensured that there would be a Scout on the radio at all times that night. I walked outside with MacGillivary and looked up at the night descending over the desert, saying, "I think we're good now."

He replied, "It's definitely dark enough," folding his arms and gazing at faint lights on the western horizon.

In such wide-open desert, most of the nights were 100 percent illumination—meaning, the moon was almost always bright enough so that we didn't need to use our night-vision goggles as we patrolled through the desert west of the Euphrates.

Back inside our Scouts' hootch now, we told the teams, "Get your shit and saddle up; we're moving out now." The men grabbed their rifles and weapons, with their ghillie suits rolled up on their packs. (We weren't wearing our ghillie suits because we really didn't need them, but we had them ready, if necessary.)

With our gear on, we moved outside. I confirmed with MacGillivary and Howerton where our teams would be, and went over our contingency plans should any of us take fire; for instance, if Howerton's team were to take fire, they were to break contact, haul ass, and move to the closest support team. That way, had Howerton's or MacGillivary's teams taken fire, my team would have supported them with substantial heavy fire. We decided that the team that had to move the farthest, near the far northwestern edge of the open desert, always left first.

We were operating in pure open desert to the north and west, with a main highway running northwest to southeast, bordering our main area of operations. Task Force 1Panther had ordered us to keep "eyes-on recon," eyeballing the main roads near the desert. We were scoping for Saddam's convoy. Howerton's team left first, followed by mine, with MacGillivary's team holding tail-end Charlie. Our teams moved in ten-minute intervals; that night, about twenty minutes passed between the time Howerton's team left the wire to the time MacGillivary's team moved out.

As my team started to move, going outside the wire, we had to immediately peel right off into the sand in order to maintain our stealth. I could see dogs everywhere in the desert. I knew these animals would be our biggest problem, as they indeed proved to be during our nearly three months west of the Euphrates. A dog, especially a wild dog in the desert, can easily compromise you and your men and get you killed quickly. In Sniper School, we'd been taught how to deal with being tracked by a dog. In the end, if you're able to move away from a dog, or around one, that is your best course of action. After many experiments, I found the best way to get rid of a barking dog in combat was to shine the infrared laser, known as the PEQ-2 Alpha, in the dog's eyes. The infrared would burn his eyes and he'd run away, allowing us to keep our cover and maintain noise discipline.

Once we'd pushed off into the desert, moving in the shadows beneath a wall of the compound, staying in the black, our patrol became much more challenging because just 50 meters in front of us was a main road. Cars, trucks, and motorcycles were rolling by in both directions on the road. Many times, we'd lay as flat as we could, right next to the road, to keep from being seen by headlights. I got the timing of the traffic down, and told my team to get ready. One by one, we sprinted across the road. It seemed to take forever, but we kept running until we'd reached the cover of rubble and rocks on the other side, dropping down into the sand.

I took point and we moved north. We headed toward our assigned hide sites—mounds of sand in the desert where we draped desert camouflage netting over us and hunkered down on desert reconnaissance. We called in our desert recon hides to Howerton and MacGillivary, updating our field intelligence every two hours. As with nearly all of our reconnaissance missions in the desert, we stayed out nearly until sunup.

It was a quiet first night, and we got in the wire clean, our covert movement undetected. The only movement we had seen was farmers about 700 meters away from my team. Some nights the farmers would build a bonfire near their farmhouse, and I could see their sheep and donkeys in the glow of the firelight. It was easy to see clearly in the stark desert. Strangely enough, the farmhouse had Christmas lights strung all around its roof. It was a regular Gypsy camp.

I remember another night of desert reconnaissance in the same area. We noticed that the "Gypsy Palace" (my team's name for the farmhouse) had started to get quite a few visitors, all men. I told Arroyo to get on the horn and tell our Scouts' HQ that we were on the move. "Tell our guys we're going in for a closer look, and to be on the lookout for enemy." My team picked up and moved toward the highway, playing the "Dodge the Headlights, Dodge the Car" game, crossing one by one to the rubble and rocks on the other side.

We stopped suddenly as three men came out of the Gypsy Palace to have a smoke around the fire. As I looked down, we were sitting ankle-deep in mud; fortunately, shadows from mounds to our left kept us in darkness. The night sky was lit up by a full moon. Hunched over, I slowly started to walk toward the farmers' fields, to the rear of the Gypsy Palace. We weren't spotted, and set up in a cornfield inside a furrow. I was in a sitting firing position, as Bailor and Arroyo covered my left and right flanks, respectively. I was carrying my SR-25. We were just 75 meters from the back door of the farmhouse.

Three hours later, the three men were still sitting and talking around the fire, smoking and drinking tea. I remember feeling close enough to reach out and touch them with my knife. I could see the ash dropping off their cigarettes through my Leupold scope. A couple times, a man would rise up from the fire and start walking toward the cornfields. Each time, as he moved in our direction, I'd raise my barrel, ready to engage as he'd walk toward us. He'd stop 15 meters from us to take a piss. Then, he'd walk back and join the Gypsy Camp festivities. Once the party was over and they went inside to go to bed, we slowly moved, low-crawling directly behind us, to get into the shadows and dogleg back around into the desert near the Gypsy Camp.

Ready to cross the highway again, I got on the horn and told the other teams we were going to cross. Each team heard me and said, "Roger, we've got security for you." And fortunately, we crossed safely, staying undetected.

In our hide sites for the rest of the night, I remember laying in the prone behind my rifle, when all of a sudden, out of nowhere, the temperature dropped drastically, to about 40 degrees Fahrenheit. This was bone-chillingly cold for us, as we were all acclimatized to 140 degrees Fahrenheit, even in that early November. The sudden cold front coming in without warning rocked us. Our teeth chattered, and without any cold-weather gear on that night, it was challenging just holding on to our rifles.

I remember thinking that I was going to freeze to death that night. I knew that I had to get Arroyo and Bailor warm, and told them, "Get ready to move." We patrolled around to keep warm, staying active, stopping periodically to take a knee. I made sure that Howerton and MacGillivary knew that my team was up and moving, and I continued to keep my guys very active. It was the only alternative to freezing, and thank God, it worked.

Anytime I patrolled at night, I made sure that my team had infrared (IR) strobe lights in their pockets, ready to pull out, activate, and keep us from being fired on by Coalition fighter jets, bombers, or helicopters. There had been a lot of confusion on who was who at night, and I didn't want my team to become the next statistic.

During that cold night patrol on foot through the desert, the ground seemed uneven. Looking down, I realized that we'd ended up in the middle of a vast graveyard, mounds covering the sand in all directions. We all took a knee. Bailor and Arroyo sipped from their CamelBaks, talking about how spooky it was, and I said to them, "Hey, at least winter's here." Looking around at all the grave mounds under the full moon west of the Euphrates, two things crossed my mind: These graves could contain all the bodies that magically disappeared every time the Coalition was in a firefight in this area, or this could simply be a local graveyard. There was no mosque nearby, nor any other sign that it was a religious burial ground. Moreover, the graves had no markings on them of any kind. Either way, I added it to my field intelligence.

By now, it was long past midnight, and I told my team to saddle up and move out. We headed back to the Rad Site. Patrolling back to the wire, I stopped my team in the shadows near some rubble and took a knee, seeing what appeared to be an abandoned compound 200 meters north of the Rad Site. I could see people with AK-47 Kalashnikov assault rifles moving in the abandoned compound.

We sat there for ten minutes, carrying out reconnaissance, the silhouettes of their Kalashnikovs easily detected. I thought to myself, *That's interesting. No daylight movement at all; they must only come alive at night around here.* As we continued walking back to the wire, Arroyo called ahead to let the two front towers know our team was coming in while staying in the shadows. Once we were about to cross the road to go back inside the wire, I noticed the red dot of a laser right on my sternum. I knew immediately that the laser was coming from the two front watchtowers, from the clueless paratroopers on guard duty that night. The next step, once you've set your red laser on someone at night, is to shoot and kill them.

"Take a knee," I said to my team. I stood in the open, pissed off, with the laser still on me. Pulling my radio out of my vest quickly, I tuned in to the towers' frequencies and said, "This is Hawk3. If you don't take that laser off my chest, I'm gonna give you a reason to shoot."

"Oh, sorry—we thought you were one of them," an ignorant paratrooper replied. His voice was nonchalant and blasé, like he was eating potato chips and watching a football game on television stateside.

"We will be crossing the road now. If I see any lasers, I'm coming to pay you a visit."

"Roger," the paratrooper replied, and the laser disappeared.

It was hard to believe that our own paratroopers could not distinguish 82nd Airborne Scouts and snipers from the insurgents; furthermore, all of the paratrooper guards on the watchtowers that night had been explicitly told that our Scouts would be going out the wire, on desert reconnaissance, and coming back in the wire before daybreak. This clearly reflected poorly on the paratroopers' leadership, which was also a real problem at Volturno and St. Mere. It was marked by ineffective dissemination of information, and, to put it bluntly, total communication breakdowns. Failure to communicate in war leads to your own men getting killed by your own men, and every time that happens, you've just done your enemy a huge favor.

Once back in the wire, I told my team to head to the hootch while I went to the tower that had nearly lit me up. I told the paratrooper on guard, who seemed like he'd just woken up, "If I ever hear or see you guys lighting up any of us with lasers again, I swear on my life, I will cut you where you sleep." Shamefaced and crestfallen, he was too shocked to reply. He wouldn't look me in my eyes. As I turned to walk away, he began apologizing. I stopped, turned around, and said to him, "There's no room for apologies in war. You better get your head out of your ass and realize where you're at. This isn't some fuckin' video game you can pause whenever you feel like. This is the real deal."

Once back in our Scouts' hootch, I went to Lieutenant Swartwood and gave him all my field intelligence on the Gypsy Palace, the burial ground, and the now-active abandoned compound. "Good job," he said.

I replied, "Thanks. Oh, and by the way, sir, if you could re-explain to whoever is guarding the towers that we are on their side, I'd greatly appreciate it."

He cocked his head to one side, frowning and looking at me with a puzzled expression on his face. "What do you mean?" he asked.

"It's kind of hard to come back in the wire with lasers on your chest," I said, and his eyes nearly popped out of his head.

"Unreal," he replied, shaking his head, his hands on his hips. "I'll take care of it."

Walking away toward my cot, I said to him, "Roger that, sir."

Hanging my gear up near my cot, I was still disgruntled. *Not only do I have to worry about the enemy; now I've got to worry about being shot outside the wire by our own paratroopers.* I dug out all my cold-weather gear and said to my team, "Who knows, guys, maybe we'll have a white winter in Western Iraq!" Arroyo laughed, and I said, "Just wait, Arroyo—if we get a blizzard, you can eat the yellow snow."

Arroyo replied, in his fashion, "That's fucked up, Sergeant."

We later learned that the abandoned compound was a copper factory, which was a big treasure in Iraq. Hell, I once saw an Iraqi kill another Iraqi with an AK-47 over some rebar. My first instinct was that "the night crew," the local Iraqi Arabs, were scrounging for anything left over or taking over the place.

We had actually made plans to fully infiltrate the compound at night by silently taking out the roaming guards with knives. We wanted to conduct a recon of what outfit was operating there, why, and gather any intelligence we could, but word never came down the pipeline with a green light. Who knows; maybe somebody got cold feet, which was starting to become a trend. Word on the street was that our lieutenant denied many operations requested by various Special Ops who wanted sniper teams, because they were deemed too dangerous, and he didn't want to be responsible for anyone dying under his command. When I heard that, I smirked and said, "He should be in politics; he's already got the deny-to-gain mentality. Hell, I think he'd be good at it, probably even be our president one day." I walked away, shaking my head.

A couple weeks later, with many desert reconnaissance missions under our belts, we had the most pleasant Thanksgiving in a war zone that I can recall, although in truth, the fare was not exactly five-star cuisine, and it certainly wasn't the kind of place I'd take someone on a first date.

President Bush, however, had decided that he needed a date with rear echelon troops in Baghdad, whose desert camouflage uniforms had never been out the wire. I remember thinking that this was his way of showing appreciation for our combat extension. I was wrong. Like all other line units in Iraq, we were ignored by

1/75 Rangers being Rangers. Top row, 3rd from left,
PFC Joe LeBleu, 1999

Combat ops at the Rad Site

Far right Spc. Joe LeBleu in 1/75 Rangers, 2002

Firing the .50 cal sniper rifle

Going to the Mayor's Compound, downtown Fallujah

Me as a private first class in 1/75 Ranger Regiment

Humvee recon at the Rad Site

Moving up a steep mountain on combat ops with 1/75 Rangers

On top of Mayor's rooftop pulling security with the .50 cal sniper rifle

My squad in 1/75 Rangers

Raiding a village with air support in Kabul

U.S. Army Sniper School, 2003

our commander in chief on his dog-and-pony show that Thanksgiving. While he served hot steaming turkey with gravy and all the trimmings in Baghdad, we at the Rad Site chowed down on one meatball with rice in the middle of it. I looked down at my plate on Thanksgiving, and back at the cook, saying, "Well hell, I don't know if I can eat all that! How about you give me a real culinary challenge and toss me two meatballs!"

The cook said to me, his face serious like he was doing me a favor, "Sorry, Sergeant; everybody gets only one meatball. There's not enough for two." I'd heard earlier that CNN and FOX television channels were showing Bush and the infamous Thanksgiving dinner in Baghdad, and I reckoned that Americans watching those telecasts back home actually believed that all of us in combat in Iraq were eating that way, which was as far from the truth as you could get. Bush was parading around like he was doing us a favor, right after he'd extended our combat tours. He'd given little justification for us to continue fighting in the middle of a guerrilla war which he had no plan to fight and win, and the reality for us at the Rad Site was that our food rations were scarce.

Almost every night, our platoon leader, Lieutenant Swartwood, and our sniper team leaders—Howerton, MacGillivary, Martin, McGuire, and myself would not eat hot rations with our men, so that our men could eat more. We would open MREs (meals ready to eat), or snack out of care packages. We weren't looking for recognition or sympathy, but we knew that was what a leader should do: always put his men before himself, and never put his men through anything that he would not go through himself. As the Ranger Creed states, "110 percent and then some."

Missions like our first desert reconnaissance night mission at the Rad Site became quite regular, nearly every night. Most all of our missions were quiet. Or, as I liked to say many times, "We are beating a dead horse out here." The temperature kept dropping; it was definitely winter in Iraq. We could see our breath at night, and the skies were dark and cloudless deep in the desert, making it seem like it was freezing cold. We dug out our cold-weather sleeping bags, kept the coffee and hot cocoa brewing at all times, and did anything we could to keep our minds off the Rad Site shithole we were stuck in, with no return date set to get back to Volturno.

On December 5, 2003, a new friend joined our family—Mike Tucker. All we knew about him was that he was there to write a book on the war. We were all fairly skeptical at first, thinking that he might compromise our missions, but he turned out to be a valuable asset on desert reconnaissance, and we discovered that he had a lot of clandestine experience in Burma, which helped us on reconnaissance west of the Euphrates.

He set up his gear in Lopez's room and that night, the insurgents welcomed him with a mortar barrage of 81mm rounds. I remember it quite well, because just like every night, getting hit with a few mortars was routine. But that particular night of December 5, I counted thirty-three mortars hitting inside the compound. When the mortars began hitting around us, MacGillivary and myself, not caring anymore about the mortar attacks, stood and watched through the heavy rain as enemy 81mm rounds rained down.

As everyone else rushed inside, I turned to MacGillivary and said, "Do you want a cigar?" He just looked at me and grinned.

After a few minutes, I said, "Okay, this is fun," and I went back inside. After the mortars had stopped—which seemed to take forever—we got on the horn real quick and found out that miraculously, no one in the entire compound had been hit. Lieutenant Swartwood came out of the shower room we'd built inside the hootch, a towel wrapped around his waist and covered in water. Shaking, and with his eyes bulging out, he rushed to his room. At that moment, all of us broke out laughing, busting our guts to find out that he'd hidden in the corner of the shower during the whole attack. In reality, there was nothing else you could do, but being that he was our platoon leader, we found our comedy, as we always did, within each other.

Shortly after the last mortar round had hit us, we got a call from a watchtower. A paratrooper guard had seen the flash from an enemy mortar tube directly in front of the compound, to the east. We were going out that night anyway, so given the current field intelligence, we changed our patrol plan to recon the area to the east, where the flash from enemy mortar tubes had been sighted. "Roger, we'll check it out," we replied to the watchtower. But we never found the tubes, nor the base plates, as a monsoon-like rain blackened the desert and drenched us on our mobile reconnaissance patrol that night.

Soon after, we got word that the Scouts needed to do a daylight reconnaissance mission, to gain field intelligence on insurgent activities in the desert near the Rad Site. Our night operations had been successful enough to warrant a shift to daylight ops, now. It was early December, and the hunt for Saddam was still going full-swing throughout all of Iraq.

To switch over from night to day on desert reconnaissance is risky business; there's a very sure bet of being compromised when shifting gears that quickly in combat. They are two distinctly different worlds: Daylight recon focuses on people's daylight routines, road traffic, and the normal desert activities of shepherds and goatherds. Night recon, on the other hand, is a situation where most people are inside their homes. It's more than likely that the only people outside their houses in a guerrilla war are either up to no good, or insurgents.

Hence, daylight recon is more difficult, in terms of who to look for and who to ignore. This is where scanning techniques are crucial, because now you are dealing with mixed crowds that could contain some insurgents. For instance, we got field intelligence around this time that any male Iraqi wearing running shoes and a *dishdasha* was an RPG triggerman, because he could hide the launcher and grenade underneath his man dress, and with the lightweight running shoes on, easily beat feet and escape.

On our first day of daylight desert recon, we inserted two hours before sunrise so we could get to our hide sites unnoticed, before the shepherds and goatherds got up. Waiting in the darkness for the sun to come up over the desert, I was miserably cold; it was the coldest I'd ever been in Western Iraq. As the sun peeked over the eastern horizon, I said to Bailor and Arroyo, "It's about time; let's get this rodeo started," thinking to myself that I couldn't wait for the sun to warm my body. The sun was bright and gold to the east of us now, lighting up the open, empty desert. It revealed a scene that was new to us, even though we'd lived in the same world every night.

We could smell fresh bread being made nearby, and donkeys and sheep were waking up for their morning foraging. Lying in our hide sites, we could hear roads and jeep trails in the distance filling up with cars and trucks and motorcycles. The scent of sheep grew stronger as great flocks passed by us. Shepherds shouted out in Arabic to each other, and to the unshorn sheep with their thick, grayish-white woolly hides. Within an hour, we had sheep and farmers within feet of our location. We stayed covert, unseen and unheard. Even though the sheep were within arm's reach of us at times, they never looked us in the eye and gave no indication that they knew we were there. I whispered to Bailor at one point, "Those sheep are damn lucky that I'm not hungry right now." He nodded, smiling back at me.

Arroyo got on the horn, in whisper mode, and updated the other teams in our area. "Be aware that shepherds are out with their flocks."

"Roger," they replied.

The flocks soon disappeared to our south, dust clouding over the sheep, as we continued to focus on daytime reconnaissance west of the Euphrates, especially on the Gypsy Palace, the haven for believed insurgent activity that we'd grown to love.

With our ghillie tops on, our upper bodies blended in with the scrub brush. We had also strung desert camouflage netting over us, and the bushes gave us excellent concealment. Our rifles were covered in Bowflage paint, making our sniper rifles the same color as the desert, breaking up their outline and making them blend in; barrels, scopes, and stocks, each rifle was completely covered in desert shades of camo paint.

Hours passed and the daily routine of farmers and shepherds continued; at that point, there was no sign of suspicious activity by any locals in the desert. I could hear the goats and sheep returning to their farms. Some of the goats returned to the Gypsy Palace. Farmers lit up smokes, and after a few more hours of desert reconnaissance, Bailor said to me, "I'm gonna go down for a closer look," and he low-crawled down to the bottom of our berm. He stopped behind a bush, getting eyes-on recon on the ramshackle mud huts and cinder-block houses in front of us.

Arroyo crawled behind him, carrying a camouflaged M4/ M203, to pull security for Bailor. I stayed on top of the berm with my M24 sniper rifle, scanning the road and surrounding houses, north to south along the desert horizon. With the sun above us now, at high noon, the warmth was comfortable, and most definitely, long awaited. About thirty minutes went by, when out of nowhere, I heard a swishing noise behind me; it was the sound of feet moving through sand, at my seven o' clock, slightly behind me and to the left.

I assumed it was Bailor, coming up around from his quick recon, when I rolled slightly on my right side, in the prone. I had my rifle set up directly in front of me, on its bipod legs. As I turned to see where the sound was coming from, the top part of a red-checkered *khaffiyeh* came into view. Definitely much closer than I'd ever wanted to be with one; the man's head was completely wrapped, ninja-style, in the red *khaffiyeh*, with only his eyes exposed. Dressed all in black, I could also see the wooden buttstock of an AK-47 Kalashnikov in his arms, carried at the low ready, without a strap. He froze in place. Caught in a cold death stare, we were communicating with our eyes, as in, *Holy shit, where did you come from?*

At the same time, I eyed his weapon and knew I was lying on my sidearm, attached to my right thigh. I realized at that moment that it would be impossible to pull my sidearm out of its holster and get a shot off at him. I also knew that I'd lose the fight if I grabbed my rifle, set up on bipods right in front of me. I even thought of my closest knife, but I remembered you should never bring a knife to a gunfight. All he had to do, in one second, was rotate and pull the trigger. However, I would have to grab my weapon, maneuver, point, and shoot, which takes a minimum of three seconds.

With all that in mind, I knew that this was it. For a fleeting second, I couldn't believe that out of all the combat I'd survived, this was the way I was going to go out. What seemed like an eternity probably only lasted thirty seconds; everything was moving in slow motion. Suddenly, he disappeared, like a ninja. *He just gave me a free pass*, I thought. He could've easily taken me out, but for some reason, he didn't. I thought I understood: He knew who I was by the type of rifle I was carrying. He knew what I was there to do in his country.

I grabbed my sniper rifle the quickest I've ever grabbed it and stared down my barrel between his shoulder blades as he ran away through the desert. *Since he gave me a pass, I'll give him a pass. I'm sure we'll meet up again soon, to pay our debts.* I lowered my rifle as I watched him disappear into the city known as Watertown, named for the many water tanks and towers throughout.

That was the day I should have been decomposing on the side of the berm. Within five minutes, Bailor and Arroyo returned to the top of the berm, next to me, and I told them about the recent appearance of the red ninja. Bailor said to me, "No shit—are you serious?"

"Unfortunately." I paused, and we were all quiet for a while. After a spell, I said, "How did your eyes-on recon go—because apparently, you missed one."

"There was no movement to the front of us. Where the hell did he come from?"

"Well, I'm working on that," I replied, still feeling very grateful to be alive and still wondering why the red ninja had given me a free pass. There was no need to inform the other teams or Command, since I'd watched him disappear into the town.

Throughout the rest of the day, we all sat in silence, carrying out our reconnaissance, as my mind raced and I sat uneasy, with an eerie feeling all around me. *Today should have been the last day of my life.*

Dusk came on, our desert recon now at about fourteen hours, and darkness began to set in, along with its bone-chilling desert cold. Once it was pitch black, we picked up and began to move south to our extraction point, calling in our exfil as we moved out through the desert so that our SUVs would be there waiting for us, ready for an immediate pickup. We sped down the road to our compound, headlights off, and rolled inside the wire to our hootch. Getting out, exhausted and moving slowly, I said in a low voice to my team, "That was one helluva day. I can't wait to see what tomorrow has in store for us. Never a dull moment at the Rad Site."

To this day, the face of the red ninja haunts my sleep.

As the nights grew colder in the desert and the missions on foot grew longer, we hadn't much evidence that Saddam was in our area. Being out at the Rad Site, we were always the last ones to get current field intelligence from Volturno, regardless. In mid-December 2003, I was sitting outside the hootch, waiting for our mission brief for that night, when Lopez walked up to me and said, "We got him. Saddam was captured yesterday." I remember thinking, *Well, that's great. We're going home now.* And then, I realized that it was open game now that the head chair at the table for the next ruler of Iraq was up for grabs.

I walked back inside the hootch. You could hear all of the Scouts talking excitedly about Saddam's capture, and then, talking about going home. This quickly changed as we found out that not only were we not going home, but we would also be staying longer in Fallujah and Western Iraq, and we still had no date set to go back to Volturno.

The fighting would soon increase dramatically. *Things just keep getting better*, I remember thinking.

Standing outside the Scouts' hootch in late December 2003, warming our hands over a huge fire in the night, MacGillivary and I heard a loud, percussive boom followed by rifle fire. "That can't be good," I said to MacGillivary. He just kept staring southeast, as the gunfire increased. I realized that the Iraqi Santa Claus had brought us a unique gift just before Christmas Day. It was colder than hell and our teeth were chattering like runaway trains. We were not on a mission profile that night, and we'd expected to cool out and relax for the first time in a few weeks. Within seconds, we got a call on the horn: A paratroopers' Humvee in our sector had been hit by a strategically placed IED, in a coordinated ambush just two miles from the Rad Site.

I remember asking, "Any KIAs?" as I latched on my flak jacket and vest, thinking it was quite possible we'd lost some comrades.

"No, none that we know of yet," our radio watch answered.

The insurgents had set up a box ambush, with IEDs at the north and south ends of an intersection, with both IEDs set to blow at the same time. Luckily, only one IED had actually gone off, or else everyone in the paratroopers' convoy would've been dead. Within minutes of the call, we had all of our gear on, knowing we'd need sniper teams out there to secure the burning Humvee. I remember thinking, in the midst of all the chaos, how well our sniper teams had gelled over the past few months. We had to issue very few verbal commands; it was almost like we were reading each other's minds, and could predict the next movement. We were really tight and together.

Before we even had our vests all the way on, we were rolling out the wire. Once we'd left the Rad Site, teams automatically covered each other's fields of fire, our rifles outboard as we neared the flaming Humvee.

I said out loud, "We need to get there quick, because people are going to be able to see these flames for miles. It's a prime opportunity for our enemy." We were flooring it to get there, now, really pushing the Humvee to its max. As we rolled up on the crash site, all sniper teams were briefed on where to go and where to set up security. Before my Humvee even stopped, we were filing out the back, Arroyo and Bailor leaping out with me.

With the burning Humvee secured, MacGillivary and I started pushing our sniper teams south about 50 meters, in a half-moon formation. We both knew that a Ma Deuce was still mounted on the burning Humvee and loaded with a box of .50 caliber ammunition, the linked ammo running down out of the heavy machine gun. We didn't have much choice; we couldn't push out too far without losing our ability to secure the burning Humvee. At the same time, we couldn't stay too close, as the intense heat from the flames would cause those .50 cal rounds to "cook off." Sure enough, just seconds after pushing across the road, the fireworks began, with .50 cal rounds crashing through the night, going off everywhere.

As the rounds were going off, I yelled to our sniper teams over the firecracker-like explosions, "Make sure you're pulling security, looking for anyone still moving, anyone still in the area!" You could feel the heat from the burning Humvee. The flames kicked up like a huge bonfire on a winter's night. All of our night-vision gear was rendered useless by the flames of the torched Humvee. We might as well have been staring into the headlights of a car with its high beams on.

I told Bailor, "Keep eyes on the top of the dirt mound," which was off to our right, about 10 feet high and perhaps 10 meters away from us. I sent a message down the line to all sniper teams: "Keep in mind that anyone can see these flames from miles away. Stay sharp and look for any kind of movement."

Once all the .50 cal rounds had cooked off, and the fire was starting to lessen somewhat, MacGillivary and I started walking toward the flaming Humvee to ensure there were no KIAs inside, or any equipment that might have been left within. Scanning the inside of the flaming Humvee, we could see charred radios, two M4s, the black plastic completely melted off, and a pair of night-vision goggles, destroyed. The tires were nothing but piles of black rubber. Only the charred black metal of the wheel wells remained, sitting on the sand. The Humvee was completely black, the seats melted down so that only burnt, exposed springs were left. The scent of burning rubber was thick in the air, almost like an oil refinery smell. The hood was busted open from the blast of the IED, and you could tell that's where the fire had started, once the engine had gone up in flames. The windshield was cracked from the blast.

Eyeballing the abandoned assault rifles, I turned and said to MacGillivary, "What the hell? This can't be right."

MacGillivary smirked and said, "Yeah, that was smart."

"Probably not the best strategy in the world to fight the enemy, but then again, this war is changing, isn't it?" I said. We found out later that when the Humvee had been ambushed, the paratroopers had run north into the wide open desert, without any weapons.

With the fire almost out now, we started patrolling slowly along the road as darkness descended. We were looking for any other IEDs that had not gone off, known as unexploded ordnance. Zigzagging across the road, back and forth, MacGillivary found a wire and said calmly, "Stop."

I froze in place. "What do you got?"

He replied, "A wire."

I turned toward him, watching him follow the wire south to the edge of the road. Our teams maintained security for us as we followed the wire all the way to the end and realized it really was Christmas. In the midst of the ambush, the wire had become disconnected from a car battery, used to initiate the charge for the IED blasts. That is why the second IED in the ambush did not go off.

Rifles at the ready, we followed the wire up the 10-foot-high dirt berm, ensuring that no insurgents were still hiding and that the area was clear of enemy. At the top of the berm, we found more car batteries, more wire, and expended 7.62 brass from AK-47 Kalashnikovs. From the markings in the dirt, we could easily tell there had been five to six insurgents. There were also two RPG grenades; you could tell that the RPGs were the insurgents' reloading cache. Following the trail of the insurgents' footprints down the backside of the berm, we found a dirt road 100 meters away. I could see truck tracks deep in the road, and wagered that this had been the insurgents' escape route.

I linked back up with MacGillivary on top of the berm, being careful not to disturb the RPGs, which we thought may have been booby-trapped. Taking a knee, we looked down on the ambush site, scanning left and right down the road, trying to visualize how the insurgents had set off the coordinated ambush. Sitting there for a couple minutes, the scent of burning rubber still thick in the desert night, I said, "They're getting smarter."

He nodded, his face hard, looking west across the sands.

We headed back to our teams to tell them to call in a "sit rep" (a situation report) and to get a head count. But our teams had already done that. We got the update on the horn that all paratroopers in the ambush were alive and accounted for, including the paratroopers who'd abandoned their M4s.

We called Explosive Ordnance Disposal to send out a team to secure the RPGs and check out the site. As the fire died down, the intense desert cold swept over us. It was hard to stay still. It seemed like it took all night before the EOD team arrived; their usual response time was two hours, but that night was an exception. Finally the EOD team showed up. They walked up the berm like they had better places to be, grabbed the two RPGs without checking for booby traps, picked them up, carried them to the back of their armored Humvee, placed them in the back, and got in and rolled away without even so much as a "by your leave." I guess we'd interrupted their movie schedule that night. I said to my team, "Well hell, I could've done that four hours ago."

Without any imminent threat, there was no reason for our snipers to be there any longer. We rolled back to the Rad Site before sunup. A squad of paratroopers then pulled security until a U.S. Army tow truck arrived after sunrise and hauled the charred ruins of the Humvee back inside the Rad Site compound. Just like all forward bases, they had commissioned the locals to do the everyday routine work for a little extra cash. Once again, this led us back to the same problem we'd faced in the beginning, of letting locals work inside the wire with no background checks. I had always been suspicious of the Iraqi trashmen who would come into the compound to empty all the trash. I would even follow them around. Something just didn't seem right one day, so we stopped them on the way out to do a search. We found many envelopes containing the addresses of soldiers' families back in the States. Who knows what they were planning, or who they were spying for; they easily could have sent anthrax to those addresses. We apprehended the three men and turned them over to the military police for interrogation.

I can't say I was surprised, as I'd predicted this since day one, but what really set me off was that I specifically remember telling everybody I talked to in that compound to burn all mail. This was another example of the clueless mentality demonstrated by the watchtower soldiers who had pointed their red lasers at me that night.

Having been lucky enough to enjoy the deluxe Thanksgiving dinner at the Rad Site, I wondered what sort of splendid Christmas dinner we would have. We spent the holiday season at the Rad Site, through Christmas and New Year's, and continued freezing on night missions past New Year's Day. Finally, the day we'd all been waiting for came around: We got the word that we were going back to Volturno in mid-January.

Our return convoy was somewhat challenging; heading back to the Euphrates and the eastern shores of that majestic river, the SUV I was in kept stalling out, as if it wasn't bad enough that it was a white vehicle, a dead giveaway that Americans were in the area. "I hope we move quickly," I said to one of the other Scouts, who was my passenger, "because if we get ambushed or hit with an IED, it's over. An IED will cut right through this vehicle like a knife through butter." Needless to say, the whole time I was driving back with our convoy to Volturno, I was on edge.

Back at Volturno, thank God in one piece, I dropped off the SUV at the Tactical Operations Center, for mission use, and jumped in the back of the snipers' Humvee. We headed back to our Scouts' hootch, a long-awaited return to our home away from home.

A sandstorm greeted us that day, the first in a series that hit us for the rest of January. We were also hit like clockwork with storms of a metallic sort, shrapnel and bullets and RPGs and IEDs, throughout January and February 2004. Back at our old stomping grounds in Fallujah, we engaged in far more action than we had seen in September and October. We did so many missions once back at Volturno, I wouldn't even know where to start. Put it this way: If we were at a bar and you asked me, "So, you were in Fallujah? I'll bet you saw a lot of action," I could only say, "If I were to tell you about all the action I saw, just in January and February 2004 alone, we would need two weeks and a bottle that never emptied."

The next day, Lopez briefed us that we were going to start doing security missions for the mayor of Fallujah. With Saddam captured, there had been a dramatic increase of insurgent activity in Fallujah; it seemed like every cell that had been asleep was awake now. We were hit with regular IED ambushes during our security runs for the mayor. Our ears started bleeding from the many IED attacks, and migraines became a daily occurrence.

I remember going to a field medic on Volturno with a couple other snipers, complaining of the constant ringing in our ears and the severe headaches, caused by the daily IED attacks. The medic just shrugged and said, "Here—take some Ranger candy and drink some water. You'll be all right." Rangers always referred to Motrin 800 as "Ranger candy" because we took it on a daily basis, for all the aches and pains our bodies were forced to endure.

Facing the turn in the guerrilla war in Fallujah, I realized by mid-January that my worst prediction had come true: We were now neck-deep in a political war. We were all growing very tired of being attacked and stabbed in the back by the very same people we were sworn to protect. Out of nowhere, political meetings were popping up all over Fallujah, with security convoys from Task Force 1Panther guarding Lieutenant Colonel Brian Drinkwine and his staff each time they'd meet with the sheikhs, imams, and the mayor of Fallujah, throughout January. These meetings all turned out to be decoys for strategic IED ambushes on the paratroopers and other elements attached to Coalition forces. The leaders of Fallujah used these meetings as a way to lure Drinkwine and his staff into the city so that Iraqi insurgents could ambush them (along with the security convoy guarding Task Force 1Panther command and staff) with IEDs, RPGs, and small arms.

I now knew that I was fighting a dirty war. I was guarding our enemies against our friends. We were sick of the political games being played on our behalf while our lives were on the line. We didn't know what we were fighting for anymore. Luckily for me, as a sniper, I had the ultimate negotiating tool. Not many people in the world can say no to a sniper rifle at 1,000 meters.

Things came to a head during the Valentine's Day Massacre, not unlike what went down in Chicago when Al Capone gave out his Valentine's Day gifts on February 14, 1928. Although folks in Fallujah spoke various Arabic dialects, their language of corruption and violence was much the same as that spoken in the American Midwest in the 1920s.

We heard a loud boom near eight in the morning on Valentine's Day. I looked over the wall and could see a huge cloud of black smoke mushrooming from the heart of Fallujah. "Hope that wasn't any of our boys," I said to our teams. Almost all of us were standing on a table, looking over the wall now. Seconds later, machine-gun fire erupted throughout downtown Fallujah, deafening in the desert morning. Word came quickly to get snipers downtown.

We geared up, tossing our body armor and helmets on as we hustled to our Humvees. After the twenty-two IEDs in January, I'd resigned my position as driver. We'd gotten hit so often from IEDs since our return to Volturno that we didn't even flinch anymore. We had reached the point where every IED that hit us only made us more aggressive and more pissed-off, as if we didn't even feel the shrapnel flying by us. I'd always say when an IED went off near us, "Who gives a shit. There'll be another one, so let's go see what's for chow."

We just didn't care about living anymore. We were so tired of fighting a faceless war that fattened the pockets of our government at our expense. If you knew how much profit our government, and especially Bush and Cheney, were making off this war, you'd be sick to your stomachs. Not to mention all the illegal things KBR and Halliburton are getting away with, while Cheney is the CEO. How ironic. After a while, many of us were hoping that something would happen to us, just so we could go to Germany for ice cream.

Rolling into Fallujah, I looked at my spotter, Private First Class Chris Knouse, age twenty, from Sarasota, Florida, and said, "Look for anything suspicious—windows, doors, alleys, rooftops, corners—and look hard for RPGs."

McGuire, sitting across from me, grinned and said, "I love coming out the wire with you."

"Why's that?" I said, shouting over the gunfire.

"Because you always get our minds ready for what we're about to enter."

I turned back and gave him a half-smile, thinking, *I reckon I've done something right over here.* Gunfire echoed throughout Fallujah. The mayor's building had burned to the ground, and black smoke drifted heavily overhead as we rolled up on the main drag. You could see blood in the streets. Dead Iraqis lay on the sidewalks, and the scent of raw sewage was stronger than ever. Machine-gun fire rattled in the distance.

Once we discovered that the mayor was alive, we secured the area around the ashes of his compound and drove him to a safe house in Fallujah. Before we moved the mayor, I'd said that we needed to relocate him across the river, but whoever made the decision to move him decided that a mile down the road would suffice. I was frustrated by this bizarre and wrong-headed choice for the mayor's new office. The mayor's new house was the only building within an enclosed compound, and it was right next to a soccer field and what appeared to be an elementary school. When the insurgents moved to attack the mayor again, this would dramatically raise casualties, with many innocent children being killed.

Nevertheless, the mayor was secured, so the Scouts got the order to return to Volturno. As we drove back, I scanned the area for photographic Intel and made sure that my team did the same, in preparation for the next time we'd be called out.

Back in the wire, fortunately with no one wounded or killed, we came to find out that an Iraqi police lieutenant had walked up to a high-ranking member of the mayor's detail and blown his brains out with a sidearm. Then, the police officer had opened the back door for Iraqi insurgents to waltz in and commence their own very bloody rendition of the infamous Valentine's Day Massacre.

A few nights later we received an Intel report on a known location of the "Mad Mortarman," the one who'd kept us company for so long with his 81mm and 105mm artillery shells. We headed to the location in the early morning, well before sunup, our hands gloved against the cold, *khaffiyehs* wrapped around our necks. As the sun came up over the desert, I remarked to Arroyo, "Put out a VS17 panel," which was a daytime recognition signal to all friendly air assets, such as helicopters and fighter jets, to let them know that friendly forces were operating in the area.

We'd seized the family's house, the house of the Mad Mortarman, and told the man inside, "We need you and your family to stay here today." We knew that if we released anyone from the family, we'd immediately be compromised—"The Americans are at the house!" We'd also made the decision that if anyone were to visit, we'd keep them there as well. We knew that our only chance of catching the Mad Mortarman was with the element of surprise; we needed everything in the neighborhood to be hunky-dory, with no hiccups.

The family fed us tea and bread, and they remained hospitable and gracious throughout the day. We had no altercations or issues with them, and the man of the house was very resourceful and helpful as to the Mad Mortarman's whereabouts. We heard gunfire echoing back and forth throughout Fallujah, but this was not our fight that day; we were totally focused on taking down the Mad Mortarman. Our extension was coming to an end. With our impending redeployment back to North Carolina on the horizon, I guess you could call it a going-away present.

Long Rifle

We watched the sun go down, never once seeing the Mad Mortarman. After eighteen hours on the rooftop, we called for our extraction, and came to find out there would be no exfil at that time. The paratroopers had decided it was too risky to extract us, due to the many IED ambushes and mortar attacks taking place throughout Fallujah. Even as we sat, freezing, and in complete darkness on the roof that winter night, we could see the insurgent mortars raining down on Volturno, as had been the case every night—although the enemy mortar tubes were nowhere in sight from the rooftop we held.

Volturno kept turning down our requests for extraction, telling us we had to wait it out until things quieted down. We couldn't afford to wait much longer, however. Throughout the day, many visitors had arrived, and now there were just over thirty people downstairs, with many cars parked outside. It was starting to get obvious that something was up in the neighborhood. We knew we had to move before our second sunrise on the roof. By now, it was almost four in the morning. We considered beating feet and extracting ourselves, patrolling back to Volturno, but first, we decided to attempt one last radio call for extraction.

When we called Volturno, we were told to hold our position— they were five mikes out. We all looked toward Volturno to confirm their movement toward us, and through our night-vision goggles, there appeared a convoy of Humvees headed straight for us. "Roger, holding position. Look for IR strobe," we replied to Volturno, as the infrared strobe was our nighttime signaling device.

"Roger, we got you, headed your way," Volturno replied, and we all breathed a very heavy and collective sigh of relief.

Getting out of the freezing cold, we headed downstairs to the crowded house, the scent of burning kerosene stagnant in the air. Though we'd had no altercations for the past eighteen hours, and were grateful for the family's hospitality, we remained some-what on edge, especially toward the older males who had come by throughout the day. We suspected they were insurgents.

We moved 100 meters away from the house, in the shadows, as the Humvees rolled up to us. There was no specific order; we just jumped in the Humvee closest to us, anxious to get out of the cold. Climbing into my thick, cold-weather sleeping bag that early morning was a blessing.

Although the days and nights seemed to pass slowly as we contin-ued to go on mission after mission, at long last, we had our rede-ployment date set. We were told we'd return to North Carolina in mid-March. *We've already been extended once*, I thought. *I'll believe it when I'm on the bird, flying home.*

The days were warming up as we headed into March. Sand-storms frequently covered the desert like a blanket, even blacking out the sky at times. Marines were now starting to fill Volturno, as they were our relief. We had the pleasure of meeting the first Marine Scout snipers in Volturno. We had arranged to take them out on a leaders' recon to show them what they were up against and what to expect. We took the Marine Scout snipers out at night, to get them attuned to night activity in Fallujah and to get a feel for the terrain in the darkness. We explained that people in Fallujah were aware of the curfews in effect, and that they should not be outside their houses past certain hours or else they would be declared insurgents.

We also took them out during the day so they could get a better understanding of daylight activities in Fallujah. We briefed them on insurgent activity, showing them buildings they could use and buildings they should stay away from. We wanted the Marine Scout snipers to have as much field intelligence about Fallujah as we could give them, of both the daytime and the nighttime worlds. We didn't want them to walk into a war they knew nothing about, like we'd had to do seven months earlier.

The downtime we shared together with the Marine Scout snipers on Volturno was intriguing, as we spent some time cross-training. We gained an appreciation for their Scout/Sniper School and their tactics. I have always said to my snipers, "Anytime you can learn something new, especially from an outside source, take full advantage of it," and we certainly did with the Marine Scout snipers. Likewise, they didn't hesitate to learn from us, and were genuinely interested in our tactics and our knowledge of Fallujah and Western Iraq.

As more and more Marines filled Volturno, I became aware of opinions from Marine colonels and generals about how they thought we'd been too aggressive—that we were going about fighting in Fallujah all wrong. I remember laughing to myself, thinking, *Everyone has an opinion until they pick up a rifle and dodge that first bullet, and then that opinion turns into survival mode.* I felt sorry for the Marines, because they were in for one hell of a fight if they tried to do anything differently from the way we'd been doing it. At that time, we had Fallujah in a good place. Right before we handed it over to the Marines, we were doing active day and night missions throughout Fallujah. Up until the last minute, we were extraordinarily busy, never hesitating to enter Fallujah.

The most crucial missions for us took place in those first couple of weeks in March. As I told my team, "It's always in the end that you get hurt. Your mentality overall starts to change, knowing that you're going home, and you lose your combat edge." Every day before we'd go out on a day mission, followed by a night mission, I'd tell my team, "We're not even close to going home yet—keep the same mentality that has kept you alive this whole time." I liked to call this period, "The Last Mile."

Coming off our last mission in Fallujah, we shook the hands of the Marine Scout snipers and said, "Keep your head low, and good luck." They thanked us. As I walked away, I said to them, "It's all yours, boys."

The way we were set up to go home was that the married guys would go home first, and then the single guys would trail on the next plane. I didn't like that idea at first, because any kind of a good leader takes care of his men first, then himself. Especially on a battlefield. At that point, though, it really didn't matter, being that the Marines were taking over.

We waited for the darkest hour on a moonless night and then rolled on trucks to Baghdad International Airport, the cold night air whipping around us. The deep darkness meant we would be less prone to attack. I realized that after surviving all of those IED ambushes on Humvees, we were now rolling on our convoy to the airport in regular five-ton, open-bed trucks, with nothing to protect us from RPGs, IEDS, small arms, or any other insurgent attacks—nothing but the bodies of our buddies seated next to us.

We laid low, pulling security outboard, leaning back on each other, keeping as low as possible and aiming our rifles out in all directions. After what seemed like forever, the night wind cutting right through our bones and our hands frozen on our rifles, we found ourselves rolling under streetlights and past massive stone villas. We knew we'd finally reached Baghdad. We pulled into the airport and rested in Quonset huts for about twenty-eight hours before boarding C-130s in the middle of the night. As we waited, I knew we were not home free yet. Everyone kept telling us, "It's over for now," but even though we were surrounded by friendlies, I kept my team mentally ready for combat.

After seven months of intense combat, it was still surreal to us that we would not be going on any more missions; the adrenaline high we'd been living on, and surviving by, still controlled our bodies. As always, I wanted my men to keep that high, and to always be aware of where they were at—a war zone. I told them, "Don't worry; if we make this flight out of Baghdad, you can relax." Many planes and helicopters had been shot down as they were taking off, so just because we were flying out of Baghdad didn't mean we were out of the reach of enemy fire.

Word came in the middle of the night to stand by with all of our gear so we could board the C-130 quickly. Once we got the green light, we all moved as one, quickly running up the ramp into the plane in single file. They never shut off the engine because they knew what waited for them out in the desert. They wanted to get out of Dodge as quickly as possible.

As we strapped down into the bird, I stared out at the dark horizon, at what had been hell—and my home—for so long. We sat there under red lights, blacked out as the ramp began to close, making the black horizon shrink until it disappeared completely, and making the whole situation seem like a bad nightmare. The C-130 began speeding down the runway, propellers growing louder as we began to pull up aggressively, almost as if we were going to shoot straight up. The pilot was clearly taking premature evasive action in case an insurgent was sitting out there with an RPG with our names on it. I remember talking to God, saying with my eyes closed, "Sure would appreciate it if you could help us out of here."

I looked up across the bird at the men, their desire to make it out alive written plainly on their faces. We all just sat there, waiting for the boom to bring us out of the sky. I kept looking behind me out of a small window to see our climb in altitude; once we'd cleared 20,000 feet, I knew we were home free. I looked at our guys and just grinned as I fell back into my seat, taking off my helmet. I knew now that I was on the freedom bird; I was really on my way home.

As we disappeared into the night toward Kuwait, I couldn't help but think how different everything would be now. I have returned from many missions, but nothing like what we had all just survived. I knew I was desperately looking forward to a toilet that flushed and a bed filled with the warmth of my wife.

Once we hit Kuwait, we were held over for eight hours. I remember walking through "Tent City," looking around and saying, "So this is how the other half lives." We had time to grab a quick bite to eat before we were wheels up, so we walked into the chow hall, skeptical of what we'd find there since we were so used to getting scraps. The moment we walked in, we were amazed to see how many different types of food were available. They had everything you'd find at a mall food court, even ice cream. We stood there with our jaws open.

"This has got to be some kind of mirage, right?" I said. (We were in a desert, after all.) "Now I know why we never had any food . . . It was all here!" We scattered throughout that chow hall as if we were running for cover in a mortar attack, and we stuffed ourselves until we couldn't talk (although I was disappointed not to find any meatballs).

Everybody we met there, those who had never gone past Kuwait, stared at us as if we had just survived hell. We would walk together as a group, our uniforms tattered from combat and bleached from the Iraqi sun, while everyone around us wore brand-new uniforms. I didn't mind the stares. I wanted them to see the soldiers who'd had the balls to fight on the front lines instead of hiding in the rear, which so many did but will never admit.

A few hours later, after being able to relax, not having to look forward to our nightly routine of mortars, we got word to stand by for a new bird. They wanted us to switch planes from the military C-130 to a civilian World Airways 747, which was smart. We were still at war, after all (even though this wasn't as obvious in Kuwait). Plus, a little bit of luxury on the ride home wouldn't hurt.

We loaded the plane and were soon wheels up, headed back to the beautiful (and very green) Fort Bragg, North Carolina. The plane was full of cheerful soldiers, and deservedly so. We all

spoke of our memories of home—girlfriends, wives, children—
all of whom seemed so distant, even though we were on our way
home to them. We did a side stop in Ireland to refuel, where we
all yelled, "We've come for your lager!" With the plane refueled,
we all became more and more anxious as we grew closer to the
States. Having lived in hell for so long, we didn't really know what
to expect. We were feeding off the very memories that had kept
us sane and given each of us our own reasons to fight and survive.

Everybody calls war hell, but what you call hell, we called home.

The pilot of the World Airways 747 came over the intercom
in America, saying, "Welcome home, boys." I'll forever remember everyone cheering and clapping as we stood up with a look of
ecstasy and gratitude on our faces. I'll never forget the overwhelming feeling of flying into Pope Air Force Base, North Carolina, and
the pure ecstasy and joy of knowing we'd survived war in Iraq—just
being so damn glad to be alive and in one piece. But at the same
time, I also experienced a quiet, humble feeling of grateful pride,
knowing that I'd brought my whole team home alive from the war.

As the wheels hit the tarmac, we again applauded and a few
guys yelled, "Whoa, it's beer-thirty!" Although it seemed like we'd
been away from home for an eternity, it ended in a heartbeat; as the
doors opened to North Carolina sunlight on an early spring day,
all the combat faded away like a bad dream. A fresh spring breeze
blowing through the pine trees welcomed us home. We knew we
were alive and in America.

As we began to file out of the plane, we were overwhelmed
by all the colors, the banners welcoming us home, the redbrick
buildings, the many varied shades and hues of people's clothing,

and everywhere we looked, greenery. We were so accustomed to no color, except for the sand—Iraq had been a panorama of white, gray, black, and shades of brown and tan. White and gray men's clothes, and black clothes for the women. And the terrain in Iraq: all brown and tan, day skies either totally blue or winter gray and black. So it was kind of shocking, at first, to see so many various colors in the bright daylight of the American South.

We filed off the plane into a formation, with cheering and applause echoing around us. Families and loved ones were shouting the names of paratroopers and snipers. As we stood there, trying to take it all in, I looked over to my team and said, "This is it, boys. We finished the last mile. Welcome home." I shook their hands. Arroyo and Knouse smiled and nodded to me; they understood my appreciation for their professionalism, and the overall good job they'd done as Scouts and snipers in Iraq. We moved as one toward the hangar, which was roaring with the noise of families and loved ones. I could see my wife Natalie in the crowd. She almost seemed like a stranger to my eyes. We weren't used to seeing American women, so beautiful and smelling so good and looking like heaven.

We were called to attention and released for ten minutes, so we could talk with our loved ones before we had to load the buses and return to the barracks to put away our equipment. I ran into Natalie's arms and held her close, kissing her. I introduced her to my guys, my team, and to their girlfriends. She informed me of the disturbing troubles she'd endured over the past four hours. It seems that the 82nd Airborne had me listed on two separate flight manifests. There was some confusion as to which plane I'd been on, and in fact, my name wasn't even included on the manifest for the flight I'd actually taken. But in the end, Natalie was in my arms and I was home. That was the undisputed truth; the flight manifest was the last thing on my mind. The only thing on my mind at that moment was . . . well, that's just none of your business. Some things are better left unsaid.

I came to find out I would only be home for five months. Afghanistan beckoned. We got orders for far Afghan hills within a month of being home from Iraq.

I remember watching CNN on our barracks television during the first week of April, within a couple of weeks of being back home. It felt unreal to watch Marine infantry digging foxholes outside of the Cloverleaf in Fallujah. I couldn't believe my eyes. That's when we heard the Marines had lost their foothold in Fallujah, and had been pushed out of the city by insurgents and terrorists.

I remembered how the Marine leadership had said that the 82nd was too aggressive when we held Fallujah, and that the Marines would creep in like fog on the insurgents and terrorists in Fallujah, taking a very different approach than the one our paratroopers had used. I closed my eyes and shook my head, thinking of what Mike Tucker had said to 1st Marine Division intelligence just six weeks earlier: "If you think that not killing your enemy in Fallujah is the answer, then you and your men are in for a world of hurt."

*Why don't they ever listen?* I thought. Well, now they were going to learn the hard way. In the days to come, this is exactly what happened, as more and more Marines were killed. I also learned that the sniper team we'd taken on leaders' recon—showing them what not to do in Fallujah and what to stay away from—

had all been wiped out when they ignored our warnings and went to a house known for its high enemy activity. One night, believing they were safe in that house, they had all gone to sleep. Insurgents crept in and killed them all.

I felt very let down throughout that spring and summer of 2004, because it seemed that everything we'd done to secure Fallujah had been in vain. We had worked hard to ensure that Al-Qaeda, the Black Flags Brigades, and other terrorist and insurgent groups did not gain control over Fallujah; everything we'd sweated and bled for was now a faded memory. I also saw Blackwater security contractors, dismembered and burned, hanging from the steel girders of the oldest bridge crossing the Euphrates in Fallujah. Our Scouts had just patrolled there, only three weeks earlier. I couldn't help but say to myself, *What the hell is going on now, in Fallujah?*

Even Kurdish *peshmerga* commanders up north, and Kurdish intelligence officers, were strongly questioning what had happened to Fallujah under Marine command, pointedly asking Mike Tucker on April 1, 2004, in Dahuk, Kurdistan (northern Iraq), "How did the Marines lose Fallujah in four days?"

## Book Two:
# Far Afghan Hills

A FEW MONTHS LATER, WE FLEW INTO BAGRAM AIR FORCE BASE NEAR Kabul in early September 2004. It seemed way too early to be putting on desert battle dress uniforms again. I felt like I'd just taken them off. Walking off the World Airways 747, I could see snow-capped mountains of the Hindu Kush surrounding us at all points of the compass. I immediately felt that this location—being in this depression with mountains all around us—made for an easy target. It was quite sunny, but not hot, with cool breezes flowing off the mountains. It felt like springtime, even though it was September. It was nowhere near the extreme temperatures we'd endured in Iraq.

The air in Afghanistan was much thinner than in Iraq, with Kabul and the valley there at 5,000 feet and the nearby mountains ranging from 8,000 to 10,000 feet. The ridgelines and ranges were incredibly dry, much like the mountains in Nevada: treeless, sandy, and very rocky and rugged. As in Iraq, the air was thick with the stench of raw sewage, diesel fumes, and other pungent aromas. (I noticed that body odor in Afghanistan was much worse than in Iraq—as if they hadn't bathed in years.)

I always tell people now, "If you ever want to know what the earth looked like when Jesus walked the earth, go to Afghanistan." Clear, cobalt-blue skies flooded the horizons, with very few clouds floating over the rocky peaks. I remember thinking that if the skies stayed cloudless like that, it was going to be a very cold night—and it always was. Afghanistan was unbearable at night, stark, freezing cold, the type of cold where you just don't want to move, or even breathe.

Lopez had picked up his First Sergeant (E-8) before we'd swooped for Afghanistan, and he'd requested that I be attached to Charlie Company. He knew I was getting out of the army in June of 2005, and he'd said to me, "Look, since you're getting out, why don't you join us at Charlie Company and be our sniper—help our paratroopers out with tactics and all your Special Ops knowledge."

"Sure, I've got no problem with that," I replied.

So Charlie Company, 1st Platoon, became my new family. To tell you the truth, I don't think I had much of a choice in the matter. I was used to getting adopted, being attached to everybody and their mother, because of my background and experience in Special Operations. Now I was among folks like Sergeant First Class Mike Lahoda, platoon sergeant for Charlie Company 1st Platoon, also a school-qualified sniper. We would often lean on each other for opinions and advice. I had the pleasure of meeting Lahoda when I first arrived at Fort Bragg, and also in Iraq, where our paths crossed on occasion. The platoon leader was 1st Lieutenant Jason Dumpser; fairly new to combat, he listened well (most of the time) and was a pretty good lieutenant.

These days, I carried a wooden-stocked M14 with a Leupold 10x scope, a decent sniper rifle, lethal and accurate out to 800 meters in mountain terrain such as that found in Afghanistan. With a match-grade barrel, it's solid out to 1,000 meters. The M14 fires the NATO round, 7.62x51, same as the M24 sniper rifle. A rifle with great stopping power, it was favored by Marine infantry and many U.S. Army infantry in Vietnam, and it's still used by many people in Special Operations.

Carrying our rifles slung barrel down over our shoulders, we moved to an open-bay tent and set up our gear. Having lived through many cold desert nights in Western Iraq, we were familiar with the routine. I pulled out all my cold-weather gear first, and lined my cot with my thick, black, cold-weather sleeping bag, and rearranged my ruck so that all my cold-weather gear was on top, for easy access during night missions.

In Afghanistan, three years after Al-Qaeda's attacks on the American homeland, I was first and foremost concerned with staying alive and keeping the paratroopers around me alive. Even though I was now in the place where the war against the U.S. had been planned, and where it had started, I was even more aware that I was back on the ground where the blood of my brothers had been spilled. This alone had me focused and enraged, ready to return the favor. At this point it had become personal to me. I wanted to avenge my brothers because I know they would have done the same for me. Every time I would gear up for a mission or patrol through the lovely mountains and valleys of Afghanistan, I always had Crose, Anderson, and Commons in mind. Each time I went out the wire, I would say to myself, "Now it's my turn."

I'd completed countless combat missions in Special Operations, and now, I was a combat sniper veteran. I remember thinking in Afghanistan, *It's not so surreal anymore; it's just another day at the office.* I knew we were in Afghanistan for a historic mission:

to secure the first national elections ever held in that country. President Hamid Karzai's personal security had been at grave risk since the spring of 2002, with some of his most trusted and closest advisors assassinated in Kabul. Karzai, of course, was one of the leading candidates in the running to rule Afghanistan during that fall of 2004. Our mission, then, to ensure that the national elections went off without a hitch, came at one more difficult fork in the road for Afghanistan, a country whose people had known little but war for the last thirty years.

Night and day, we patrolled through Afghan villages, talking with the village elders, handing out flyers, and trying to get field intelligence on Al-Qaeda and the Taliban. Of course, elders and villagers alike were scared to speak due to the threat of being beheaded by the Taliban and Al-Qaeda if they were in any way deemed to be informants, so we really got nowhere on our village patrols.

In that short tour, three missions stand out in my mind from Afghanistan.

The first was an early-morning mission, rolling out the gate in the gray predawn darkness. Afghans crowded around the gate—it looked like a swap meet—very crowded, with Afghan men, some in turbans, wearing long, baggy *dishdashas* over trousers and battered, torn leather vests, bunching up around the gates and clamoring for work on the base. Going outside the wire was like fighting traffic in downtown New York.

Once free of the crowd, we rolled into our first city, a village roughly a mile from the base. We stopped in the middle of the road to let Afghans cross. Looking to my left, an eerie feeling came over me as I saw four Afghan men holding AK-47 Kalashnikovs with banana magazines jacked in. They stared at me, grinning in a hateful manner—what we call in America a "smartass grin"—only 10 meters away from me. They wore green camouflage uniforms with multicolored badges sewn on their sleeves. Once again, nobody had given us any field intelligence before we'd gone out the wire on any Afghans dressed like these men, carrying AK-47s. Sitting in the back of the Humvee without doors, I stared into the eyes of the four men, with my rifle laid across my lap, barrel pointed toward them. I suddenly pushed forward my safety lever inside the trigger well of my M14. My rifle was set live now, and I laid my finger on the stock, above the trigger, so it wasn't obvious.

I started to picture in my mind who to take out first if anything went down, but I knew not to fire right away, as we were third in the convoy. If they were enemy, they would've likely fired on the first vehicle. As I watched them, I could tell by the way they were talking with the locals, at ease among their fellow Afghans, that they were obviously welcome. But being stared at by four guys with AK-47s just 10 meters away still didn't sit easy with me. I made mental notes, and as I'd done in Iraq, I stored away a photographic memory recon of the village.

We continued our staring contest, like we hated each other. I said to the driver of our Humvee, without taking my eyes off of them, "How much longer are we going to sit here?"

"Not long. We'll be moving in a second," he replied.

"Good. Because I've got four guys with AKs staring at me, and I have no idea who they are."

A paratrooper riding shotgun said, "Those are the village police, the local security."

"Don't you think that's something everybody should have known before we rolled out the wire?"

"Oh, so nobody told you?" he said, sarcastically.

"Well, if somebody *had* told me then I would've known, wouldn't I?" I immediately found out that Charlie Company had no communication whatsoever, and this was just one of many problems to come. *I'm really starting to regret my transfer*, I thought at the time.

The convoy started to move now, and as we slowly pulled forward, I waved at the four village cops, and smiled at them. They just kept staring at me, eyeing my rifle. I could still feel their eyes on my back as we rolled on through the village, and I knew that the word would spread that American snipers were in the area. I made a mental note to be prepared, and base my actions on the fact that the enemy was aware of my presence.

As we drove on toward the next village, I remember thinking to myself how close that had been to the situation with the red ninja in the Iraq desert. Now, at first glance, it may not appear to some folks that it was in the same league as my brush with death in Western Iraq. However, that same eerie feeling was present. I had no cover, I was in a naked Humvee, and for those four Afghans, armed AK-47s, killing me would've been like shooting fish in a barrel. So all I could do was smile because yet again, I'd cheated death.

We arrived at our second village, and poverty was everywhere—kids without shoes or even rags to wrap around their feet, sunken, weathered faces all around us, and mud huts the most-common residences. Mud was the only sealant available for the Afghans to lay between roof beams (actually, sticks and scavenged wood), and plants and wild grass were growing out of many of the roofs. Just like any village that we came to, the streets suddenly filled with Afghans, children playing in the dirt, their faces marred with dried mud, as the boys offered us hash: "Five bucks, *hasheesh*, hash, five bucks, *hasheesh*," the dark, oily hashish rolled up in torpedo cigarette form. We pushed these boys away, focusing on the mission at hand, which was to gain field intelligence on Taliban and Al-Qaeda, and pass out flyers for the elections that November.

The sun was really bright now as it neared high noon. We all had to wear dark sunglasses, not only to protect our eyes from the harsh glare of the sun but also, from the constant stream of dust all around us. As in all Afghan villages, goats and sheep clogged the streets, and you could smell the god-awful scent of raw sewage in the air. It was clear this country had focused on little else but war. The total lack of investment in schools, health clinics, sanitation, and social welfare could not be ignored.

As I did in every village, I would always distance myself from the rest of 1st Platoon so that I could have eyes on the surrounding areas. Not being surrounded by paratroopers gave me the ability to scan the crowds and sense any potential danger to my fellow paratroopers, while simultaneously eyeballing the dirt roads leading in and out of the village.

"LeBleu!" Lahoda yelled now, and I ran over to him. He was kneeling next to a berm that overlooked farm fields, the furrows bare. *This is all too familiar*, I thought as I ran to him. It felt like the ambush in Fallujah a year earlier when I'd made the 1,100-meter shot. Everything felt the same. Closing on him, I slowed down my breathing to prepare for a shot.

"Five hundred meters out, two men in a field," he said to me as he eyeballed the field with naked-eye vision.

I took a knee and raised my rifle, looking through my scope. I could see no mortar tubes, no rifles, no munitions of any kind, nor vehicle to escape with. It was odd that they'd chosen the middle of a field in plain sight to hold their conversation. They kept glancing at the village and gesturing as they talked. I remember thinking it could have been two farmers discussing a poor harvest, or what we were doing in the village—or it could have been some kind of reconnaissance. Either way—as with any such activity in a war zone—it was nothing to take lightly.

I said to Lahoda, "Two guys talking, no weapons. But we should still check it out. Could be reconnaissance for a mortar attack, or an IED ambush."

"Yeah, all right," he said, nodding.

By now, 1st Platoon had finished talking with folks in the village and the flyers had all been handed out. Everyone moved back to the convoy of Humvees to load up and return inside the wire. We couldn't get to the two men because there were no roads leading to the field, and in Afghanistan, there were unmarked mines every five feet. It wasn't worth the risk, especially if they were simply farmers.

Afghanistan is plagued by land mines like nowhere else in the world. In the fall of 2004, land mines were as endemic to Afghanistan as the poverty I saw there. They have mines left from the Russian occupation, as well as Italian and other European mines laid by the Taliban and various Afghan warlords. On patrol in Afghanistan, you have to be especially watchful for land mines. The phrase

*Take real care* comes to mind. On our patrols there, paratroopers took small baby steps, which would slow us down and make us a prominent target in the open fields. So we'd yell at the paratroopers, "Just walk—if you step on a mine, you won't feel it anyway."

After a while, we just got used to being around land mines, and learned where—and where not—to walk. For instance, we'd be on the lookout for mines on any trails that led to the villages, and aware that basically anything off of a main road would be mined. The only potentially safe places for us on patrol were the main roads, but even there, we were still dealing with IEDs and antitank mines.

Heading slowly back toward our forward operating base, we took our time, doing a convoy patrol; this was a hasty reconnaissance to get our bearings locked on the routines and activities of the Afghans in the villages near us. We got back in the wire an hour before sundown. The early dusk was coming on, and you could feel that the dramatic drop in temperature was not far away.

A few days later, we got the word to check out another village, due to suspected Taliban and Al-Qaeda activity, and to pass out more flyers. We moved out on Humvees in the late afternoon, a few hours before the sun went down, and halted five miles from the mud huts of the village. A tremendous sandstorm hit the entire platoon as we approached the village on foot. We had to keep our heads down as we walked against the wind, the sand slamming into us. The very loose sand on the ground made it hard to walk, and while we were fighting our way through the storm, I remember thinking, *This is a prime opportunity for the enemy to hit us, because we can't see anything.*

I did my best to hold my helmet down with my left hand and to keep my right hand tight around the wooden barrel guards of my M14, well in front of the magazine. I had a 20-round magazine jacked in my sniper rifle. I looked over to Lahoda and said, "What was the point of this walk again?" and he looked back at me, aggravated, and muttered, "So we can pass out flyers." Both of us were laughing and shaking our heads now. I couldn't help but think, *So this is how we are going to win wars against the evil, radical Islamists—by passing out flyers. Sure, why not.*

Walking on, a few paratroopers behind us started to fall back, so I kept turning around and keeping my eye on them, until eventually, I walked back and took over the rear for 1st Platoon. It was clear that the paratroopers were not pulling rear security effectively, and I needed to make sure that nobody would come up behind us. You're only as fast as your slowest man. By the time we reached the village, the sandstorm had died down a little bit—enough for us to pick up our heads, glance around, and talk with each other. We were now completely covered in sand, including our gear and weapons. *Great, this is all we need—sand-covered weapons.* Everybody knows that in a gunfight, if your weapon jams, you die, and that is just what the desert sand is best at.

As 1st Platoon went into the village and began interviewing Afghans and passing out flyers, I stayed at the entrance to the village. As usual, I separated from the paratroopers to gain a better overview of the entire situation. On that day, I leaned up against the side of a house on my left shoulder, scanning the village and terrain without my scope. I could see the snowcapped mountains off in the distance, near Kabul. As the sun settled in the west, 1st

Platoon finished handing out flyers. We started to move out on a different route back to our Humvees. Although the sandstorm was over, sand still coated our weapons and gear. With darkness falling, we put on our night-vision goggles and patrolled back in a staggered formation on opposite sides of a dirt road, with the lights of distant villages glowing faintly in the early evening.

An Afghan wearing a camouflage uniform and a sidearm on his hip was with us. I presumed that he was an officer, since he was similar in appearance to the four Afghan policemen I'd seen in the other village a few days earlier. He gestured to Lieutenant Dumpser, indicating that he'd show us a quicker route. Dumpser agreed to follow him, and I said out loud, "Yeah, right—that's the oldest trick in the book for an ambush." Dumpser said, "He knows a quicker way out of here, so we've got to follow him." I turned around to all of 1st Platoon and said, "All right, men, prepare for an ambush."

The paratroopers, some of whom had not seen action with Task Force 1Panther in Western Iraq and were in their first war zone in Afghanistan, looked at me, confused and unsure of what was going on. We'd been on foot for well over five hours, walking through a sandstorm and humping rifles, water, ammo, and combat gear, and we were tired. After warning the paratroopers of an ambush, I took point for the platoon, right next to the Afghan. Watching his every move, I said to the lieutenant, "Hey, sir, if this goes down, I'm taking him out first."

The lieutenant said nothing.

"I don't know if you can understand me," I said to the Afghan, leaning over and talking right into his ear, "but if you set us up, I'm taking you out first." He looked back at me, his face blank. I was puzzled by his lack of expression. Usually when someone has no expression in a combat situation, they are ready for something to go down. We moved out, taking a bend in the road to the right, still staggered. In the middle of the bend, on the left side of the road, a two-story house appeared in the shadows. *This has got to be the ambush site*, I thought.

Not caring about noise discipline anymore, I said, "Put every single laser on that door, those windows, the rooftops, the corners— I want that house covered with lasers. And don't worry about the right side; I've got security right." Infrared lasers flooded the house as we walked by it. With the house all lit up by our lasers—which are unseen to the naked eye—I stared at the Afghan now, reading his body language. His eyes showed nothing. He just kept walking, leading us on. As the platoon cleared the bend, past the house now, we patrolled on until we reached where the Humvees were located for our exfil.

The lieutenant thanked the Afghan, as our platoon loaded up in the convoy. As I walked away from the man, I said, "You did good; you're still alive."

Rolling back toward our fire base, our temporary base for quarters, food and re-supply, and ammunition, I remember thinking, *That had to be the stupidest thing I've ever been a part of; we were just asking to get hit.*

We were also extremely lucky.

Lieutenant Dumpser had just proven a long-known adage of war to be true: People new to combat make amateur mistakes that can likely get many people under them killed. Anyone with two brain cells who has picked up a rifle at war knows that not only do you *never* let someone lead you to your death, but also, *You never trust anyone in combat except for the guy to the left and right of you. And you never trust anything in combat but your instincts.* Both of those ancient laws of war go back to the Spartans. And even those two real and distinct truths about combat are a gamble, half the time.

We rolled back in the wire that night like living ghosts, our lives spared. The Afghan cold was in effect, and our teeth were chattering and we rubbed our hands together as we slowly got out of the Humvees. Nothing was said as we moved into our open tents. Everyone started to realize what I already knew in the field—what a stupid mistake the lieutenant had made. The paratroopers laid on their cots, bone-tired, and wrapped in our sleeping bags, we all fell quickly to sleep.

As the days and nights went by that autumn, the icy cold winds carrying winter on them, we continued our operations in support of the upcoming elections. We went from village to village, passing out flyers to encourage people to vote, and at the same time, carrying out field intelligence missions on Taliban and Al-Qaeda activities close to Kabul. When the elections were a week away, we entered one of the few villages that was still new to us near Kabul. Walking into the village at about nine in the morning, I immediately noticed much larger crowds of people, almost all males, more than in any other village we'd been in. Right off the bat, this kept us on edge, knowing that with their long, baggy clothes, the Afghans could've been carrying knives, rifles, submachine guns, grenades, or suicide vests under their garments.

I separated from the paratroopers according to my usual habit, walking about 20 meters north of them. I kept eyes-on for the most likely enemy attack route, the sun bright and warm now in the mid-morning sky over Kabul. As 1st Platoon handed out flyers and talked with the village elders, they also cleared a few houses in the village and discovered weapons caches: AK-47s, RPGs and launchers, and 7.62x39mm bullets. We knew that the village elders and the villagers had lied to us, having earlier told us that there was no Taliban or Al-Qaeda presence in the village. This discovery definitely put us on edge, and we were now expecting to be attacked. We started clearing all the mud huts and ramshackle houses in the village. I stayed on the street, on overwatch, and kept carrying out reconnaissance and surveillance on the village. We'd already pulled out the men from all the buildings in the village so we could keep an eye on them while our squads searched the huts.

As I took a knee to watch the men, I noticed that a camel was walking down the street. A blanket covered the camel's hump, but it didn't have a saddle. Close enough for me to touch it, the camel ambled on down the dirt street, eventually disappearing down the road. I went back to scanning the crowd, saying out loud, "Now there's something you don't see every day."

The paratroopers found nothing in the other huts. I could see an Afghan man on a roof, fairly young—I reckoned he was about eighteen or nineteen—watching our paratroopers from a two-story house with antennas on it. It was the same house where we'd found the first cache of AK-47s and RPGs. I yelled across the street to Lahoda, "You've got a guy on a rooftop with antennas, and it's the same house that has the weapons. He's got no weapon on him, but he's scoping you guys out. Don't worry; if he makes a move, it'll be his last."

Lahoda was upset, as all Afghans in the village were supposed to be in the streets. Paratroopers quickly moved to the house and detained the young man, flex-cuffing him while Lahoda yelled at the owner, "You told me everyone was out of this house! You lied to me twice: You lied about the weapons and now, you lied again. You've got antennas on your house, and weapons, and this guy hiding up there. We'll be back to pay you a visit."

A call came over the radio right then that one of our paratrooper checkpoints up the road from us, about 200 meters, had just stopped a gas tanker. We knew that the gas tanker, quite possibly, was a suicide bomb, with the elections only a week away. The paratroopers at the checkpoint told us over the radio that they'd stopped the tanker 100 meters before it got up to the checkpoint, aiming raised M4s and M4/M203s at it and yelling for it to stop. Which it did.

As everyone moved out, I stayed in place, scanning the crowd with my M14 raised near shoulder level. Lahoda grabbed the flex-cuffed detainee and said, "You're coming with us," as the paratroopers ran and jumped on the Humvees. With everyone clear now, I kept tail-end Charlie and jumped on the last Humvee. "We're good," I shouted, latching the tow strap, and our Humvees moved as one, pulled a U-turn, and sped down the road, coming up to the rear of the gas tanker.

We all jumped out as the Humvees stopped, half of us peel-ing off left on the tight road, ditches on both sides of the road preventing our drivers from getting any farther away from the gas tanker. The rest of us peeled off right and ran up to where we had eyes on the cab of the truck.

A driver sat in the cab, alone.

Lahoda was yelling now to our interpreter, "Tell the driver to open his door, and get out with his hands up."

You could tell the driver was local—threadbare clothes, dishev-eled hair, dust all over his face, and torn-up sandals. Lahoda held his M4 on the driver as he got out of the cab—in truth, we all had a bead on him—and he stepped away from the gas tanker with his hands held high in the air. He seemed uneasy and really ner-vous, his hands and arms shaking as he walked slowly away from the tanker. Lahoda moved swiftly, grabbed him, and put him face-down on the ground.

"Search him," Lahoda said to our paratroopers. They pat-ted him down and checked him thoroughly, but found nothing. Lahoda picked the guy back up and told the interpreter, "Ask him, why is he driving this gas truck, and why is he so nervous?"

The interpreter quickly asked him in Pashto and the driver replied, close to tears, "I must do this for my family, so they won't be harmed."

The interpreter's eyes lit up now, real excited, and Lahoda asked, "What's going on?"

The interpreter said, "That truck is probably rigged as a suicide bomb, and he's said that he must do this for his family so they won't be hurt." We were very fortunate that Lahoda had been around the block before, a seasoned combat veteran, and he knew immediately what that meant. Lahoda yelled at everyone, "Get back in the Humvees—*now!*"

The whole time this was going on, I had the feeling that something wasn't right. As I scanned with my scope, back and forth over the truck, I saw wires hanging underneath the belly of the gas tank, some red, others black. I told all the paratroopers near me, "Move, move, move," and ran behind them, all of us dashing back to our Humvees. Lahoda detained the driver, so now we had two flex-cuffed detainees. We rolled back to the village with Lahoda telling everyone not to use their radios. He knew that any radio frequency from our Motorolas could set off and detonate a suicide bomb.

Once we were back at the village, Lahoda used the platoon radio—which had a closed, secure frequency and was safe to communicate on—to let our checkpoint know, "If you guys haven't figured it out yet, that truck is rigged to explode."

"Roger," they replied.

Within minutes, the paratroopers moved their checkpoint some 300 meters back, closer to another mud-hut village. The checkpoint called in EOD specialists, and we held in the place in the village. People filled the streets, going to and from the village market. I pulled out a Snickers I had been saving in my ammo pouch, opened it, and said, "Not going anywhere for a while." Lahoda just shook his head and smiled.

Within a couple of hours, by late afternoon, EOD came out and set a mobile robot with a camera on it near the gas tanker. The suicide bomb was rigged with C-4 plastic explosives and the red and black wires I'd scoped. It turned out that the wires were not attached correctly, and EOD realized they could move in and disable the suicide bomb, so they got under the tanker and cut the wires. After disassembling the suicide bomb, they gave the all-clear and we moved up to the vehicle. An EOD specialist got in the cab and drove the truck slowly off the road. The rest of the EOD team secured all of the plastic explosives and wire. Strangely, like the EOD specialists in Iraq, they never said "Thank you." I guess when you're playing with bombs all day, there's not much that needs to be said.

With our two detainees sitting in the back of a Humvee, we sped off, rolling back toward the fire base. Dusk rolled in, the sun a far distant fire falling behind the ridgelines west of us. Entering our base, we halted quickly and Lahoda dropped off the detainees at our MPs' shack to be interrogated and processed. We rolled on back to our open tents, the temperature dropping swiftly in the early dark, and dropped our gear under our cots. Lahoda and Dumpser met Lopez and gave him a quick after-action report on stopping the suicide bomber and the weapons caches found in the village.

One of the things that blew my mind over there was when we'd patrol through the mountain terrain during the day. We would mostly find abandoned fighting bunkers; while some looked freshly used, with expended 7.62 brass left behind from their AK 47s, others looked like they'd been there for quite some time. I'm assuming those older bunkers were from the days when they were fighting Russia, which, ironically, the U.S. had helped to fund. We'd also found caves, which, to my surprise, went pretty deep into the mountains. Some of the caves ran so deep that you would come up to a split to either go left or go right, which meant they continued even deeper. The others were what we called "dry holes"; in other words, a short cave. Just like any other room or hut, we cleared the caves with anxious anticipation of disturbing the Taliban's Monday-night poker game.

Inside the cave, we would switch to our night vision because of how dark the caves were. It was pure blackness; you couldn't even see your hand in front of your face. The stench of the cave was toxic. We could never figure out what the smell was or where it originated from, but the suffocating stench was bad enough to interrupt our noise discipline by making us cough. It smelled like the worst body odor mixed in with a little bit of death. I could also hear bats hovering above us at times.

Once we'd cleared the cave, we would search around for any intelligence left behind, such as maps, weapons caches, even clothing. It wasn't easy to spot a cave or bunker because they were so well camouflaged, as if they were a natural part of the mountainside. As we would exit the caves and begin our descent back to base, I would stop on a ridgeline, scouting the path ahead for any potential ambushes. While the platoon kept moving I would just sit there and look out over the mountains into the distant horizon, thinking to myself, *Funny how hell can look so beautiful.*

Afghanistan sunrises and sunsets over the many snowcapped mountains literally looked like paintings, and for those few seconds, time would stop and allow me to embrace the beauty around me. In all of combat, I found dusk to be my favorite. It seemed to be the only time of day when you could take in a fresh breath, relax, and hear your thoughts. I would always refer to it as "the calm before the storm."

Back inside the wire with the cold night setting in, I would stand outside by the tents and just scan all the mountains in a slow circle, looking for any lights or flashes—anything to indicate that there was still activity around us. Then I would do the same motion with night vision on. What I saw made me cringe inside. When I donned my night vision and scanned the surrounding mountains, I could see campfires literally all around us. I assumed many of them might be near caves. I couldn't help but think of how many of those caves we didn't see and probably walked right by.

I definitely had the feeling that we were outnumbered. Talk about "the hills have eyes"! I guess in the end, we *were* in their backyard, so I'm sure there were many trails, caves, bunkers, and key Taliban leaders we missed by not seeing what was really in front of us. Then again, we didn't have the best intelligence to work with—if we had any at all. From that point on I had a running joke at night when I'd see any campfires or lights up in the mountains. I'd say, "Hey, there goes Osama bin Laden. Do you think I'll get the reward for finding him?"

Since we had pretty much pushed most of the Taliban out of Afghanistan, there wasn't much combat going down in our immediate area—Bagram, Kabul, and the villages close to Kabul—other than IEDs placed by Taliban and Al-Qaeda. All the action at that time was on the Pakistan border—especially since there were travel tunnels that ran underneath both borders used by Taliban and Osama bin Laden as a way to escape and hide. The whole time we were dealing with the villages, our Scouts were patrolling the Pakistan border, which is just four days' forced march, on foot, from Kabul.

One night, Howerton and his sniper team were patrolling on the Pakistan border and had set up a hide site, looking for any Taliban and Al-Qaeda crossing from Pakistan into Afghanistan. Howerton had set in trip flares in his surrounding area, the flares laid in at 50 and 100 meters from his hide site in the mountains, to ensure no one could sneak up on him in the night. He also placed a Claymore mine, winding the wire back to his hide site and camouflaging it. He held the trigger for the Claymore himself. As they lay there, they heard rocks falling, scattering down the ridgelines, as if someone had disturbed the terrain.

Within moments, the trip flares went off, white flashes shooting up in the sky. The flares exposed a squad-sized element of Taliban, about six enemy in long robes and turbans, carrying weapons. Howerton set his Claymores and his team emptied two magazines rapidly at the Taliban, sixty rounds. The flares started to go out—you've only got about six seconds once a flare is tripped until the light dies—and the team changed magazines as the flares went out completely. Howerton ordered his team to break contact, which is exactly what Scouts and snipers are trained to do in that situation, and they hustled back through the mountains to a safe location, communicating to Scout platoon the contact they'd been through and their movement.

Waiting through the night, they carried out reconnaissance and surveillance in the mountains near the Pakistan border. With dawn's arrival, they moved back to their forward operating base. For his actions on that night, Sergeant John Howerton of San Antonio, Texas, received a Bronze Star. Within a week, for the first time in history, Afghanistan held its first-ever elections. Thanks in no small part to our presence, the elections went off without any disturbance or delay. It really seemed to me that we'd pushed many insurgents toward the Pakistan border during the fall of 2004.

Soon after the elections, we got orders to return home. We flew from Bagram to Pope Air Force Base at Fayetteville, via Germany, landing back in North Carolina in time for a real Thanksgiving dinner stateside—not like the lone meatball we'd enjoyed at the Rad Site just one year before.

Now back in Fayetteville, which I liked to refer to as "Fayette-Nam," because there wasn't much to do in that town and it was purely military, I remember saying to myself, *If I ever put these desert BDUs on again, it will be too soon.*

It was very calming and relaxing to be back from Afghanistan, and to be able to really enjoy all of the holidays in America for the first time in eight years. *I wish I could've spent all my holidays like this*, I remember thinking.

As my ETS (expiration term of service) date neared, I decided not to reenlist. My decision had nothing to do with my duty. I loved being a sniper more than anything else, because it ran through my veins. If there was anything that I was good at, it was being a sniper.

It was the political bullshit that had burned me out, and I wanted nothing more to do with this war. I could no longer stand to watch our leadership bed the same enemy we were fighting. As much as I wanted to stay in, I fundamentally disapproved of the new direction our military was being forced to follow. Along with many of my comrades who remain on active duty today, I object to our being forced to become friends with Al-Qaeda and the Taliban, the enemy we'd started out to kill in this war.

One thing you need to understand about a soldier: From day one in boot camp, we are being taught to kill, kill, kill. When the leadership starts to tell the soldier in combat to *stop* killing and to start rebuilding what he has just destroyed, and that he now has to become *friends* with the enemy, it really messes with his state of mind. In the long run, that causes mental problems, such as post-traumatic stress disorder (PTSD) and depression. It can also spark the blame game, making the soldier feel guilty for killing people that his leadership is now telling him to befriend. It's like having two bosses telling you two different things, pulling you in two opposite directions.

What really bothers me to this day, and no doubt will bother me until the day I die, is that we have lost our foothold in Afghanistan. Basically, we have to start back at square one, because since the autumn of 2004, we've lost one-third of the country back to the Taliban and Al-Qaeda. That tells me that the brothers I lost in Afghanistan in March of 2002, and all of the men and women who are still dying there, have died in vain. We don't even have the foothold that we won on the battlefields of Afghanistan in 2001 and 2002. Crose, Anderson, and Commons died to gain the foothold that Bush has lost.

You can't start two wars and think that you'll win either of them without even committing fully to one. The war started in Afghanistan and never ended because Bush was so anxious to retaliate against Iraq and finish what his dad had started. That whole time, we should have focused on Afghanistan, ensuring that we'd strike and kill all Taliban and Al-Qaeda where they sleep. Now, we're on a never-ending chase for Al-Qaeda terrorists worldwide, and

Taliban in Pakistan and Afghanistan, because Bush failed to focus on one war.

Feeling frustrated and downhearted in the fall of 2004, I decided that I'd had enough of our leadership failing us and leading us blindly to the slaughter. As my last months in the military flew by at Fort Bragg, North Carolina, I knew it was time for me to check out. I told all my guys, "Good luck, and keep your head down."

# BOOK THREE:
# Coming Home to Vegas

Natalie and I had packed up our house a week prior to my honorable discharge and we'd put all of our goods in storage since we'd made plans to go to Europe. It was long-awaited R & R and a great opportunity to get away with Natalie. We toured through Italy, Germany, Switzerland, and France.

Returning stateside a month later from our vacation in Europe, it was nice to reunite with Mike Tucker on Memorial Day weekend in Washington, D.C., and to see that he still had all his fingers and toes. We spent the day visiting the Vietnam War Memorial and the Korean War Memorial. We cooled out later in the day, enjoying coffee together as we discussed Mike's new book that was coming out at that time, *Among Warriors in Iraq.* We joked and smoked and had our fill of the day and when it was time to go, it was time to go. As we said our good-byes, Mike informed me that he was returning to Iraq for a combat tour with the Marines. I wished him luck, thinking of what I'd seen on the news of Marine actions in Fallujah and Western Iraq.

We parted ways and Natalie and I drove south to Florida, enjoying a little fun in the sun in Key West before we rolled on cross-country, west to the Nevada deserts and the high, rugged mountains surrounding Las Vegas—our new home. We had decided to move to Vegas, having enjoyed our visits there over the years. During my military career, I'd always come to Vegas on R & R when we'd get leave after deployments, starting in the Rangers. Our motto was, "Work hard, play hard!" Never knowing if our next mission in the Rangers would be our last, we always lived life to the fullest.

Driving into "Sin City," Natalie and I took in all the glamour of the neon lights and the casinos as if it were our first time there. I turned to her and said, "It's Vegas, baby, Vegas!" We both laughed. It was really nice, not only to be back in Vegas, but also, to be there with my wife, knowing that I'd never have to leave her again for long periods of time in combat.

Towing our U-Haul, we continued on to our new house, south of Vegas. We pulled into our driveway at around one in the morning, stretching and smiling, and saying happily, "We're in Vegas!"

I said to my wife, "Little different from FayetteNam!" She smiled a knowing smile. "Have you got all this, 'cause I'm gonna go hit the tables and take my luck for a spin," I said.

She stared at me as if I'd better not move. I might have felt like a gambling man, but Natalie had other plans for me that night. Luckily I listened to her.

"No? Well, maybe tomorrow," I said, smiling, being a smartass for once. But damn, I'd wanted to rock on the high rolling scene! Oh well . . . I knew that at the end of the day, there was just one truth about Vegas: The house always wins.

I turned the key in the front door and exploded into the house, pointing my right index finger like a gun, and began clearing all the rooms, shouting, "Room left clear, room front clear," laughing, and she just shook her head, hands on her hips. I stopped and turned back toward her, saying, "Hey, on the bright side, I don't have formation in the morning." We left almost all of our goods in our U-Haul, except for the mattress. The house smelled fresh and new and nothing like Fallujah.

In the morning, we moved everything in. It was July in Vegas and the high summer heat made me think about the desert heat in Iraq. I walked to the top of a ridgeline near my house, getting eyes-on recon on my surroundings. I could see that Vegas was one big depression surrounded by mountains, almost exactly like Kabul in Afghanistan. At the same time, I could see terrain very similar to Iraq: open desert, tumbleweeds, sand as far as every horizon line. I came to find out that Nevada, too, has sandstorms. I laughed to myself. *How ironic! I've got the best of both worlds, and no RPGs to dodge or mortars to disturb my sleep.*

I took six months off the bat, to get my head straight for "The World," as we call U.S. civilian culture, trying to get myself situated as a civilian again. The Veterans Administration (VA) registered me and processed my unemployment benefits for half a year. I kept fit, jogging and lifting weights, and hooked up with a boxing club and started sparring. (I'm still married to this day because I own a heavy bag.)

During this downtime, I weighed my future; given my background in Special Operations and my combat experience, what did I have to offer that was marketable? My ultimate long-term goal, as with many folks from the military, was to eventually get back into the U.S. government. Unfortunately, I came to find out that even with my combat experience and my unique skill set in Special Operations, I would not be selected for such a position without a college degree in hand. I thought that was ridiculous, and still do; here I am, with all this knowledge and experience earned at war against Iraqi insurgents and terrorists, and the Taliban and Al-Qaeda, but the agency in question was selecting individuals with no combat experience—in fact, with no experience whatsoever in our enemy's cultures in the Near East and Central Asia, and no tests or challenges to prove that they had sufficient on-the-spot critical thinking skills to make decisions that could ultimately save American lives.

What made things even worse was that I personally saw and worked with operators for various agencies who didn't know their head from their ass. Many times soldiers had to go and recover the "special" operators because they were lost, after having been given specific instructions on what to do and where to go when we got there; and when they would finally show up, they had to be told, "In case you were wondering, the fight is *this* way." I couldn't believe that these were the agencies' best-trained men, when even our lowliest private knew more about what was going on than they did.

But what do we know? We don't have college degrees.

All the agency in question cared about was a college degree. As you can see by the many failures in the War on Terror, all the college-degree holders are not exactly taking down Al-Qaeda, especially not now, seeing that the Taliban and Al-Qaeda have regained one-third of Afghanistan, with their bases firmly secured in Pakistan. Trust me when I tell you: A college degree is by no means a direct reflection of someone's skills, abilities, or potential. For instance, Ernest Hemingway changed the way the world writes and is regarded as one of the world's greatest authors, without having ever earned a college degree.

I do acknowledge that education is vital, but I don't feel it's of paramount importance when it comes to fighting a war. If you are not in line when God is handing out common sense, you shouldn't be in a position to make command decisions at war, or for that matter, employment decisions. I've always believed: "Until you've seen and done what I have, you don't know anything."

Disgruntled but not entirely dejected, I started taking college courses online to get the sheepskin I needed in order to check off the correct box for the agency I wanted to reapply to. Talking with many different government agencies, I was told that they'd all love to have me on board, but unfortunately, they all required a college degree.

Entering the military straight out of high school, and going all over the world on nonstop combat deployments as a Ranger in U.S. Special Operations, I never had the time to attend college classes and earn credits (like those in the regular army units do). Some of us in the military actually have to work. The only courses I had time to master were classes in jungle, swamps, mud, desert, and mountains. In six years on active duty in the Rangers and as a paratrooper sniper team leader, I'd earned a degree in survival, in endurance, in dealing with and accepting pain, in taking down my country's declared enemies, in leading men in battle and ensuring that they came home alive, and in all reconnaissance, sniping, and surveillance skills. I'd place a small bet that you're not going to find those skills in any college or university textbook, but those are the skills that have ensured the survival and freedom of this country, the United States of America, for 232 years now, and those are, indeed, the skills that will enable us to prevail in the War on Terror in our time.

While everybody was sitting in classrooms, giving their opinions and ideas on what needs to happen next in our fight against terrorism, my comrades and I were taking down the declared enemies of the United States in Iraq and Afghanistan. While some people were sitting behind computers and engaging in forums on the War on Terror, without any firsthand experience, analyzing what they in truth knew nothing about, I was making history with my brothers in the Near East and Central Asia.

I've always said, "Nobody has an opinion until they have picked up a rifle in combat." Until you've earned an opinion by being at war against Al-Qaeda, you haven't really come to a complete understanding of the history that my generation of American warriors has lived—the history we made and suffered through in Iraq and Afghanistan—in dust, sweat, and blood.

With this roadblock in my path stopping my plans to reengage Al-Qaeda from the other side of the fence—from a U.S. government position—I began thinking through my Plan B options. A good sniper always has a Plan A, and a great sniper always has a backup plan, with plenty of escape routes. Forced to put Plan B in effect, like many veterans when they get out, I took many different boring and mundane jobs. I was surrounded by kids who saw themselves as experienced and mature adults, even though the only experience they had was what they'd gained inside a classroom or cubicle.

Had I been a combat engineer or a computer technician in the U.S. Army, of course, it would have been fairly easy to transfer over to a civilian job, as these trades are quite marketable in today's American workplace. The great irony, and a damn sad truth, is that the people who are called on to stand tall at the tip of the spear in America's time of need—and indeed, in our present war of survival against Al-Qaeda—are the same people who are ignored and told to stand at the back of the line, when they are themselves in need of decent employment, having bled for our country and done their duty to ensure that America survives.

I found that my background left me with very few options: I could seek employment with the Las Vegas Police Department, or make ten bucks an hour as a Rent-a-Cop security guard at a mall, or work as a bodyguard, babysitting for a celebrity or an executive. None of these jobs really appealed to me, given that we remain at war, and my skills, background, and combat experience make me uniquely suited to fighting terrorists and ensuring that what happened on September 11, 2001, never happens again. I wasn't keen on settling for anything other than taking down Al-Qaeda; I like a challenge and I know my enemy.

After my honorable discharge, I handled a host of dead-end jobs before stumbling on an instructor's position at Front Sight Firearms Training Institute, located between Pahrump and Las Vegas. This training facility instructs people—including government agents—in defensive handgun tactics, how to handle hostage situations, and close-quarter battle (CQB) techniques. I learned about Front Sight online and contacted one of the head instructors in early February 2006.

Luckily, I was interviewed right on the phone and I got the chance to try out for the job during a four-day course of shooting and instruction blocks: You had to prove you could put it in the black and back up your résumé with actual effective instruction. It's not enough to shoot well; in order to get an instructor's position, you must also prove that you can effectively teach the art and craft of marksmanship. To be honest, I was having so much fun shooting that I forgot what I was trying out for. Fortunately, I scored high on the shooting test on handguns and rifles and showed that I could speak in front of a crowd. (The only thing I had to remind myself, when speaking, was that I wasn't talking to my sniper team, so therefore, I wasn't allowed to make anyone feel like crying themselves to sleep on their pillows.)

Once I'd finished speaking, I was invited over to talk with the head instructor. Folding his arms outside the classroom, poker-faced, he said, "Great job. How would you like to come on board and be one of the instructors?"

"Sure—I don't have anything to do tomorrow," I said, a half-smile on my face. "I guess I can teach someone how to hold a gun." He had a great sense of humor and he took it the right way, smiling at me and nodding his head. The head instructor shook my hand and said, "Welcome aboard." It was a good gig with decent pay and I was happy to have it.

He grabbed me a couple of uniforms, black BDU trousers and a gray-collared shirt with the Front Sight logo on the back. My name was on the front, as with a U.S. Army blouse, and I wore a pair of black combat boots.

All instructors carried their preferred sidearms on hip holsters. My sidearm of choice was the Glock 21, .45 caliber. Other instructors carried Glocks, while some had Colt .45 double-action semiautomatic pistols, and others carried the Smith & Wesson .45 double-action semiautomatics. Some of the instructors also carried .40 caliber semiautomatic handguns, and they would brag about how well they could shoot their 25-meter targets with their .40 calibers.

I'd go around those instructors who carried .40 caliber handguns, saying, "Well, that's a great job. I reckon anyone with a woman's handgun, not under fire, can do that. Come back to me when you put it in the black with a man's gun." I'd say this while tapping on my .45. In my book, a .40 caliber semiautomatic is not enough gun; you want a sidearm that has real stopping power to protect you and your family in your house. The .45 has more than enough power to stop any criminal dead in his tracks. Hell, I was already disappointed that I'd had to drop down to a .45 from a rifle.

I taught classes with students who ranged from a housewife who didn't believe in guns, and was picking one up for the first time in her life, to the know-it-all, wannabe rednecks standing next to the Great Almighty Government Agents (ah, the special agents who could do no wrong, and it was either their way or no way). I thought to myself quite frequently that government agents just would not listen, much like the Marines when they took over Fallujah from the army. And like the Marines, they failed. Miserably.

When it came time to do the ShootHouse—an open bay of plywood, formed into rooms just as in the ground-floor layout of a one-story house—I would stand behind a shooter who was firing live rounds from a sidearm in order to ensure his safety, as well as my own. In the live-fire scenarios in the ShootHouse, the government agents were a wreck. You'd think it was their first time ever holding a loaded weapon. A few times, I almost had to body slam a couple of them to the ground because they were so reckless. It was worse than not understanding the classic combat axiom, "Think before you move, and always, think before you shoot." They simply forgot about just one word: *Think*.

For some reason, with every bullet they shot during the live-fire ShootHouse exercises, the agents seemed to lose a little more common sense. If I had been the hostage and these agents were trying to rescue me from terrorists, I would've just told the terrorists, "Go ahead and kill me." It got to the point where I would grow tired of teaching government agents how to stay calm and think clearly under fire. A fundamental problem is that the government hadn't trained them correctly in firearms and real live-fire shooting techniques in the first place. In their various academies, such as the FBI Academy, they'd picked up a lot of bad habits.

In firearms instruction, people are always taught what's comfortable for that specific instructor, as opposed to the very pragmatic method of simply being taught the reality of what works—and what doesn't work—under fire. One thing that is vital to keep in mind is that everybody is different—for instance, in hand size, body weight, balance and coordination, and height—yet government agents are being forced to learn the same government core blocks of firearms instruction regardless of how different they are from one another, and with little or no actual correlation between that instruction on handling a sidearm under fire, versus actual combat.

The U.S. government fails to focus on what is pragmatic and effective in real-world firearms situations. One of the reasons why I was a respected and well-liked instructor was because in addition to teaching from my own experiences, I also taught my students how to handle firearms in real life. Surprisingly enough, my best students were housewives and those who'd had no previous training, which meant that they hadn't picked up any bad habits and, obviously, had absolutely no need to unlearn bad habits. With them, I was simply molding a rock into a diamond. Some of them shot even better than the government agents. They listened well and followed my instructions.

In the end, what do I know? The government agents who failed my ShootHouse had college degrees.

Front Sight shuts down in early August every year, for three months, due to the intense desert heat. In August 2006 I elected to take on a security position at Nellis Air Force Base in Las Vegas, to put bread on the table and keep the wolf from the door. Before leaving Front Sight, however, I assisted Pat Garrett in training actor Mark Wahlberg for his role as a former Marine Force Reconnaissance sniper in the film, *Shooter*. It was interesting. Wahlberg was cool, professional, and listened very well. He grasped the nuts and bolts of sniping, reconnaissance, and surveillance, right off the bat. Pat Garrett, a Marine Scout/sniper veteran of the Iraq War and another Front Sight instructor who had been hired as technical advisor on the film, taught the Marine side of sniping to Wahlberg, while I put in my two cents on the army side. Unlike most celebrities, Wahlberg was damn kind, and we greatly appreciated his genuine respect for everybody at Front Sight.

I look back now at eight years of active duty in U.S. Special Operations and as a sniper team leader and I know this for a fact: While less than 1 percent of my generation has gone in harm's way in Afghanistan and Iraq, they are my brothers forever. I will never forget their sacrifice and their blood, sweat, tears, and toil. "We few, we happy few, we band of brothers," as Shakespeare said in *Henry V* in 1600. Four hundred and eight years later, his words ring true for my generation of warriors just as they did for my great-uncle Ernie Simpson's generation in World War II.

I was able to work my way back into the U.S. government by getting a college degree, and during the process, I've seen more and more veterans of my generation returning from the war in Iraq and Afghanistan. I've watched these combat veterans as they've sought help from the VA, and I've watched as they've been turned away from jobs by the very same government they were sworn to protect and defend to the death.

For example, a Marine veteran of the Iraq War, Jonathan Schulze, was turned away by a Minnesota VA hospital in March 2007, although he'd already been diagnosed with post-traumatic stress disorder (PTSD) by his family's physician. He'd been having suicidal thoughts, so he sought help from a VA hospital in St. Cloud, Minnesota. His father and stepmother accompanied him and witnessed Schulze telling the nurse on duty that he was suicidal. Yet the VA hospital refused to admit him for treatment. Come back the next day, they told him.

Nobody tells us to come back the next day when we volunteer to go in harm's way for our country.

As CNN correspondent Anderson Cooper reported on Wednesday, March 14, 2007:

> The family says it was told the social worker who screens PTSD patients was too busy to see him. When Schulze called back the next day, his stepmom says she listened as he told the social worker he felt suicidal. The hospital then responded by telling him he was number twenty-six on the waiting list for one of twelve PTSD patient beds.
>
> In other words, he'd need to wait at least two weeks before he'd get treatment. Is that any way to respond to an [Iraq War] veteran who is telling you he's suicidal? And why, with the U.S. fighting two wars in the Middle East, are there only twelve beds reserved at this hospital for PTSD patients? The U.S. Department of Veterans Affairs expects one in five veterans will need to be treated for PTSD.

From my own experience, I believe that every veteran should be screened for PTSD, and because of the sacrifices we've all voluntarily made, no veteran should ever be turned away from VA treatment. Jonathan Schulze's dad, Jim, said, "When a vet cries out that he is suicidal, even if they had to set up a bed in the kitchen, you don't turn them away. You don't put them on a waiting list."

Four days after being turned away by the VA hospital in St. Cloud, Minnesota, Jonathan Schulze did something no Iraqi insurgent or terrorist was able to do: He ended his life. He hanged himself with an electrical cord in the basement of a friend's house.

After his death, and the deaths of other veterans who took their own lives, the VA finally decided to wake up and stop ignoring the cries for help coming from the men and women of my generation who have sacrificed so much for our country and received so little in return. It's terribly unfortunate, and just plain damn wrong, that the VA had to wait for veterans to kill themselves in order to recognize the problems that many combat veterans are experiencing when they come home from war. Why does it seem that we had no problem sacrificing our lives for our country but when we get home, we spend the rest of our lives convincing the VA that we have problems that need help. Instead of trying to fix the returning veterans, their solution is to numb us with pills. These actions dissgust me.

There is another verse from *Henry V* that comes to mind, reflecting on the VA's refusal to help Marine veteran Jonathan Schulze and so many other veterans of my generation in our time of need: "Shame, and eternal shame, nothing but shame."

It amazes me how in America, it seems that patriotism only arises when something tragic happens on our soil. As veterans, we live patriotism on a daily basis—not because we have to, but because we choose to. Words like *sacrifice* and *honor* and *integrity* are real to us in ways that our larger society will never understand, because to truly understand sacrifice, you have to sacrifice.

When September 11th went down, the worst assault ever on the American homeland, everyone was yelling "Kill, kill, kill! We want our revenge!" Well, now that we are taking our revenge against Al-Qaeda, for some ungodly reason Americans are saying, "Stop the killing. Be nice and rebuild. Invest in reconstruction aid." They're saying this while Al-Qaeda continues to cut off our heads. It feels like veterans are looked down upon for having served in Iraq and Afghanistan, yet we are the same generation hailed as our nation's saviors in the immediate aftermath of September 11th. Anytime a tragic situation happens, Americans never hesitate to call upon us. We're either loved or hated, but we're rarely respected. American culture is schizophrenic when it comes to the U.S. military, and to American veterans.

American society has been transformed into a "politically correct" culture that is ruining centuries' worth of tactics that have won many wars. You see, society can't handle the truth. That's why they have found a way to avoid facing what's really going on at war. Instead of focusing all our resources on being politically correct, we should instead focus on what we can do to achieve a positive outcome.

Since the time I've been out, I've lost jobs and been turned away from jobs because I am a combat veteran. Once my potential employers discovered that I was a combat veteran, I could see the shades go down. One security contractor actually told me, "Go and take six months and clear your head," after I'd informed them that I was a combat veteran of Iraq and Afghanistan. How are we supposed to "clear our heads" if we can't put food in our bellies and shelter over our heads, after having gone in harm's way for our country?

Keeping my professionalism, I could only reply, "It's too bad you feel that way. In case you didn't know, there is a war going on." It's scary how my generation of combat veterans is facing the same ignorance and ingratitude and lack of caring that Vietnam veterans endured. I once asked a Vietnam vet, "If you had the choice to go to Iraq or Vietnam, what would be your answer?" Immediately, without hesitation, he replied, "Vietnam." I asked him why. His reply was, "At least we had somewhere to hide." And he shook his head, frowning, and said, "You boys have got it rough over there. At least in Vietnam, we never had to make friends with the enemy." I couldn't help but agree, thinking that the jungle offers many more places to conceal and cover yourself, at war, than the desert. And in Vietnam, soldiers were allowed to do their jobs.

If you were to ask me if I would do it all again, I would tell you in a heartbeat that it's not about what you have accomplished; it's not about personal or political gain; and as soldiers and warriors, our opinions really don't matter. It all comes down to the guy on the left and the right of you, who is standing shoulder to shoulder with you in hell, staring death in the face, and refusing to take one step backwards. I knew those guys—men like Arroyo, Eggleston, Bailor, Knouse, Crose, Anderson, and Commons—my brothers. We understand the true meaning of sacrifice . . . of honor . . . of patriotism, because we have lived it.

I would fight alongside them any day.

# SIGNIFICANT ACTIONS

**March 25, 1998:** Arrived at U.S. Army boot camp at Fort Benning, Georgia. I decided to enroll in jump school because I had no contract for a specific military occupational specialty and did not want to go into mechanized infantry. Graduated boot camp on June 25, 1998.

**June 28, 1998:** Entered U.S. Army Airborne School (jump school) at Fort Benning, Georgia. Graduated jump school in late July.

**August 8, 1998–September 2, 1998: Ranger Indoctrination Program** Graduated on September 2, 1998, and joined 1st Battalion 75th Ranger Regiment at Hunter Army Air Field, Savannah, Georgia.

**September 1998–March 2001:** U.S. Special Operations, U.S. Army Rangers. All these missions remain classified, and therefore cannot be discussed within, for operational security reasons.

**January 2001:** Awarded the U.S. Army Commendation Medal (ARCOM):

FOR MERITORIOUS SERVICE AS A M249 GUNNER WHILE ASSIGNED TO ALPHA COMPANY, 1ST BATTALION, 75TH RANGER REGIMENT. SPECIALIST LEBLEU'S SELFLESS SERVICE AND OUTSTANDING PERFORMANCE REFLECTS GREAT CREDIT UPON HIMSELF, THE 75TH RANGER REGIMENT, AND THE UNITED STATES ARMY.

Also cited as the first Ranger to jump in and shoot down a missile with a Stinger antiaircraft weapon.

**March 2001–September 2001:** Honorably discharged from the Rangers and traveled cross-country in America, cooling out; sought security work, including work as a bodyguard.

**September 11, 2001:** I was supposed to have lunch that day with friends at Windows on the World, at the top of the World Trade Center. I was five blocks away, in lower Manhattan, when the first plane hit.

**Fall 2001–Winter 2001–02:** Continued to travel cross-country and ended up in Las Vegas, which became my home. Arrived in Vegas in early February 2002.

**March 2002:** Got word from a Ranger's wife about the deaths of Sergeant Bradley Crose, Specialist Marc Anderson, and Private First Class Matthew Commons on Operation Anaconda in Afghanistan. All three had served in my platoon in the Rangers. Crose was my roommate for a little while. As a specialist, I'd helped train Crose and Anderson, and briefly knew Commons. Attended and aided each funeral ceremony. After their deaths, the U.S. Army promoted both Anderson and Commons to the rank of corporal.

**March 2002–June 2002:** Lived in Savannah and helped fellow Rangers and their families; prepared to reenlist.

**June 25, 2002:** Reenlisted in U.S. Army Rangers as a Specialist, E-4.

**July 2002–January 2003:** Active duty, 1st Battalion 75th Ranger Regiment. For operational security reasons, these missions cannot be revealed.

**September 10, 2002:** Met Natalie in Las Vegas, after extended operations with the Rangers.

**December 2002:** Married Natalie at the courthouse in Savannah, Georgia.

**January 2003:** Requested to be reassigned to Fort Bragg, as a sniper and paratrooper Scout. Reported for duty with the 82nd Airborne Division. Joined the Scout platoon of 1st Battalion, 505th Parachute Infantry Regiment.

**July 5, 2003:** Reported to U.S. Army Sniper School at Fort Benning, Georgia. Qualified on M24 U.S. Army sniper rifle, which is a Remington 700 with a Leupold 10x scope, and the XM 107, the .50 caliber Barrett sniper rifle with a Leupold 4.5x14 variable power scope. Trained in all aspects of covert movement, reconnaissance, and surveillance. Also trained on counter-sniper operations and tracking.

**August 8, 2003:** Graduated U.S. Army Sniper School, with orders for Iraq.

**September 5, 2003:** Sniper team leader in Fallujah and Western Iraq; began Scout operations in support of Task Force 1Panther, commanded by Lieutenant Colonel Brian Drinkwine.

**September 2003–October 2003:** Combat actions in Fallujah. On many missions as the lone sniper from the Scouts, attached to Attack Company, 10th Mountain Division. Under fire in early October, I shot an Iraqi insurgent who was standing in the back of a moving pickup truck, from 1,100 meters in "The Boneyard" section of Fallujah. The confirmed kill was witnessed by soldiers in 10th Mountain Division and by then-Staff Sergeant Martin, paratrooper and sniper team leader, of the Scouts, who was my acting spotter. Martin is now a Sergeant First Class, in September 2007, preparing for his fifth deployment to Iraq.

**Mid-October 2003–Mid-January 2004:** Scout platoon ordered on reconnaissance and sniper missions five hours southwest of Fallujah, on the western side of the Euphrates River. October and November missions were part of overall Coalition forces hunt for Saddam Hussein, who was eventually captured by U.S. Special Operations Forces and 4th Infantry Division in Tikrit, Northern Iraq, on December 13, 2003. Based at the Radiation Site ("Rad Site"), a former Iraqi artillery factory and munitions base. Met Mike Tucker, a counterterrorism specialist and author, when he was attached to us on desert reconnaissance missions for two weeks in December 2003.

**Mid-January 2004–Mid-March 2004:** On security overwatch, as a sniper, for the mayor of Fallujah. In mid-March, the Scouts moved by truck to Taqaddum airfield and flew on to America, via Kuwait.

**April 2004–October 2004:** Regular parachute training and preparing for Afghanistan.

**September–November 2004:** On reconnaissance and sniper missions near Kabul, with Charlie Company, 1st Battalion 505th Parachute Infantry Regiment, 82nd Airborne Division, in support of the first elections in the history of Afghanistan.

**Early November 2004:** Flew from Bagram Air Force Base in Afghanistan to Pope Air Force Base, North Carolina, via Germany.

**Mid-December 2004–June 25, 2005:** NCO in charge of marksmanship classes and close-quarter battle training. I was on my way out.

**June 25, 2005:** Received honorable discharge from the U.S. Army. Took holiday throughout Europe with my wife. Reunited with Mike Tucker in Washington, D.C., on Memorial Day weekend, 2005.

**August 2005–present:** With my wife in Las Vegas, Nevada. Worked as a firearms instructor, hostage situations instructor, and close-quarter battle instructor at Front Sight Academy, where I assisted Pat Garrett in training Mark Wahlberg for his role as a sniper in the film, *Shooter*. Also, I handled high-level security for a Department of

Energy facility in Las Vegas. I now work as a bodyguard for celebrities and executives and also do security for the U.S. Air Force.

**July–September 2007:** Mike Tucker came over from Malaysia to help me write *Long Rifle*. At this time, Sergeant First Class Jason Martin gave official confirmation that he was my acting spotter under fire in Fallujah and witnessed me make the shot of an Iraqi insurgent from 1,100 meters in early October 2003 in Fallujah.

# PEOPLE

**Corporal Marc Anderson, U.S. Army Rangers:** Corporal Anderson called Brandon, Florida, home. He was thirty years old at the time of his death, at war in Afghanistan on March 4, 2002. Anderson, Crose, and Commons died on a rescue mission for U.S. Navy SEAL Neil Roberts, thirty-two, from Woodland, California. Roberts was captured and executed by Al-Qaeda.

**Corporal Matthew Commons, U.S. Army Rangers:** Corporal Matthew Commons grew up in the desert and mountains of Boulder City, Nevada. Twenty-one when he died in Afghanistan with Crose and Anderson, he was also buried with full military honors, like his Ranger comrades.

**Sergeant Bradley Crose, U.S. Army Rangers:** Sergeant Crose served in 1st Battalion 75th Ranger Regiment. Twenty-two years old when he was killed in action on Operation Anaconda in Afghanistan, on March 4, 2002, Crose grew up in Orange Park, Florida. In the late 1990s, then-Specialist Joe LeBleu helped train Crose, Anderson, and Commons, who were also killed in action with Crose on Operation Anaconda.

**Sergeant Joseph LeBleu (Snake Eyes, Long Rifle):** Sergeant Joseph LeBleu, former U.S. Army Ranger and 82nd ABN paratrooper

Scout and sniper team leader, who still holds the farthest confirmed kill of any sniper in Iraq: 1,100 meters, firing an SR-25 in early October 2003 in "The Boneyard," Fallujah. Joe LeBleu received an honorable discharge from the U.S. Army in June 2005.

# GLOSSARY

**Afghanistan, the war in Afghanistan:** A landlocked country in Central Asia, bordered to the east by Pakistan, Afghanistan's historic trading routes link Russia to the Persian Gulf, India to Europe, and China to Europe and the Near East. Invaded and conquered since the time of Alexander the Great, Afghanistan was fought over and held by the British in the nineteenth century and returned to Afghan rule in 1920.

King Zahir Shah ruled one of the few peaceful and stable eras in Afghan history, from 1928 to 1973, before he was deposed in a coup by his cousin, Mohammed Daoud. A little over six years later, on Christmas Day, 1979, Soviet tanks, fighter jets, bombers, and infantry invaded Afghanistan, the start of over thirty years of unending warfare. Radical Islamic jihadists from all over the world, principally from Saudi Arabia and North Africa, fought to end the Soviet-backed rule of the Afghan communist leader, Najibullah, and were funded by Saudi Arabian intelligence, Pakistani intelligence, and the U.S. Central Intelligence Agency, from the early 1980s to the early 1990s. Osama bin Laden, son of one of the wealthiest men in Saudi Arabia and a close friend of the Saudi royal family, recruited the Afghan jihadists for his radical Islamic terrorist transnational army, Al-Qaeda, starting in the late 1980s. (See Steve Coll's *Ghost Wars* and Lawrence Wright's magnificent *The Looming Tower*.)

The United States made a few attempts to kill Osama bin Laden and Al-Qaeda's core leadership in the 1990s, during the second Clinton administration in the U.S. (January 1997 through January 2001), but all failed. President Clinton, like President Bush (until September 11th), never ordered America's premier counterterrorists, U.S. Army Delta Force and U.S. Navy SEAL Team Six, to strike and kill Osama bin Laden, despite the fact that Delta Force and SEAL Team Six were specifically created and trained to kill terrorists.

Pakistani intelligence (ISI) has never wavered in its commitment to Al-Qaeda and the Taliban, the party that seized Kabul on September 26, 1996, and during its radical Islamic rule in Afghanistan from fall of 1996 to December 2001, routinely beheaded Afghan women for the crime of walking to a market alone. In August 2007, at the time of this writing, the Northwest Frontier of Pakistan, and Baluchistan, a Pakistan province bordering southern Afghanistan, continue to be recruiting and operations centers and armories for Al-Qaeda and the Taliban.

After the devastating Al-Qaeda assault on the American homeland on September 11, 2001, the U.S., Great Britain, Australia, and Canada led a Coalition to defeat the Taliban and Al-Qaeda in Afghanistan. Coalition forces, spearheaded by CIA paramilitary commandos, US and British Special Operations, and Australian Special Air Service, seized Kabul on December 11, 2001. Osama bin Laden managed to escape the manhunt designed to capture him, as did the Taliban's leader, Mullah Omar, and Al-Qaeda's Egyptian-born operations commander, Ayman al-Zawahiri. Since the beginning of the Iraq War in March 2003, under President Bush's command, Coalition forces have lost one-third of Afghanistan back to the Taliban and Al-Qaeda.

**Al-Qaeda:** Radical Islamic terrorist group. Main Al-Qaeda recruiting and operations centers are found in England, Egypt, Pakistan, Saudi Arabia, Syria, North Africa, Indonesia, the Philippines, Western Europe, East Africa, and all of the Near East, with the exception of Iraqi Kurdistan and Israel. The religious and financial base of Al-Qaeda is Saudi Arabia, with Pakistan running a very close second.

Al-Qaeda murders people on any continent, in any port, and at high sea, using suicide bombers who employ small boats, trucks, jet planes, cars, motorcycles, jeeps, donkey carts, and their own bodies (wearing vests packed with plastic explosive and/or TNT). The predecessor of Al-Qaeda is the ancient radical Islamic sect known as The Assassins, which likewise cited Islamic jihad as justification for its suicide attacks, and like Al-Qaeda, used terrorism as a political tool, seeking political gains through suicide attacks in the eleventh and twelfth centuries in the Near East.

Founded by the Saudi Arabian fugitive Osama bin Laden in 1988, Al-Qaeda declared war on the United States in 1996. Like the radical Islamic terrorist groups, Hamas and Hezbollah, each active since the 1970s, Al-Qaeda claims religious justification in the name of Islamic jihad for its suicide bombing attacks. *TIME* magazine reported in January 2006 that Al-Qaeda terrorists and other radical Islamic terrorists allied worldwide with Al-Qaeda now number between 50,000 and 54,000.

Sworn to destroy the United States and to kill American citizens anywhere on earth, Al-Qaeda has also sponsored or inspired many other radical Islamic terrorist attacks in the West since the devastating and barbaric September 11th attacks in America: the

March 11, 2004, railway attack in Madrid, Spain, which killed 190 people; the Al-Qaeda terrorist Richard Reid's attempt to blow up a 747 jet passenger plane; the radical Islamic terrorist bombing in Bali, targeting and killing Western tourists (primarily Australian) in October 2002; the horrific London subway and bus bombings on July 7, 2005, which killed fifty-two people and maimed and wounded hundreds more.

Al-Qaeda, at time of this writing in September 2007, remains fully committed to murdering people, including Muslims, in suicide attacks in order to achieve its political goals: the destruction of the United States, Israel, Great Britain, Australia, and all allies of the United States; the reestablishment of the Taliban as the radical Islamic ruling power in Afghanistan; and full power in Saudi Arabia, Egypt, and throughout North Africa and the Near East, with Al-Qaeda ruling Saudi Arabia directly.

**Barrett XM107:** The Barrett .50 caliber sniper's rifle. Heavy, accurate, and powerful. Not a point target weapon, like the M24 or M14, it's made to destroy engine blocks and penetrate armor. Used with a Leupold 4.5x14 variable power scope. A Canadian sniper in Afghanistan has the farthest recorded kill in combat—2,450 meters, a mile and a half—with a .50 caliber sniper rifle.

**CENTCOM:** United States Central Command. Headquarters: Tampa, Florida. Main foreign base: Qatar. U.S. military nerve center for U.S. combat operations in the Near East, Horn of Africa, Arabian Peninsula, and Central Asia.

**Command-detonated:** You see what you destroy by running a wire to the explosive and setting off the charge by hand.

**CT:** Counterterrorism. The art and craft of taking down terrorist leaders and cells.

**Delta Force:** U.S. Army Special Forces Operational Detachment Delta, Combat Applications Group (SFOD-D, CAG). Modeled on the British Army Special Air Service Brigade (SAS). Primary mission is counterterrorism. Often carries out missions with U.S. Army Rangers in support. Founded in 1977 by Colonel Charles Beckwith, U.S. Army Special Forces. With U.S. Navy SEALS, tasked with military counterterrorism (see the U.S. Army Special Forces Delta veteran and author Eric Haney's terrific book, *Inside Delta Force*).

**82nd Airborne Division:** The only U.S. military division in which parachute qualification is absolutely necessary, the 82nd Airborne is the lone surviving paratrooper division in America from WWII, when it executed four parachute assaults: North Africa, Sicily, Normandy, and Arnhem. Nicknamed "The All America Division" in WWII, because there was at least one paratrooper from every state, the 82nd Airborne is comprised of the following Parachute Infantry Regiments: 504th PIR, 505th PIR, and 325th PIR. Colonel Jeffrey Smith, Ranger/Airborne qualified, was the regimental commanding officer in Western Iraq. Colonel Smith led 505th PIR in Fallujah and Western Iraq from early September 2003 through March 27, 2004.

**Eyes on, eyeball, scope:** All terms which signify looking at something directly, and are all related to human intelligence—intelligence gained from human sources.

**Fallujah:** Historic trading, political, cultural, and religious crossroads of Western Mesopotamia. Heartland for the radical Islamic terrorist group Al-Qaeda in present-day Western Iraq. The Euphrates River borders the western edge of Fallujah. In mid-April 2003, President Bush decided not to secure Fallujah and Western Iraq, laying the groundwork for later U.S. failure there. Task Force 1 Panther—a Coalition unit comprised of 1st Battalion-505th Parachute Infantry Regiment, 82nd Airborne Division; Attack Company, 1-32, 10th Mountain Division; Delta Force commandos; U.S. Army Special Forces; and U.S. Army sappers and other attachments—raided heavily in Fallujah from early September 2003 through late March 2004, and also carried out desert reconnaissance in the hunt for Saddam Hussein, west of the Euphrates, in the late fall, 2003 (see Mike Tucker's book, *Among Warriors In Iraq*).

Four days after relieving the 82nd Airborne in Fallujah, 1st Marine Expeditionary Force lost Fallujah to insurgents and terrorists, including Al-Qaeda, on April 1, 2003. From mid-April 2004 to late November 2004, Fallujah was governed by Al-Qaeda in Iraq and other terrorists and insurgents. In the Second Battle of Fallujah, November 2004, the Marines won back Fallujah, then appointed Al-Qaeda–connected sheikhs to the Fallujah City Council in December 2004. The Bush administration continues to sign U.S. State Department reconstruction aid contracts with Al-Qaeda–connected sheikhs in Fallujah at the time of this writing, in September 2007. Al-Qaeda has regained control of every mosque in Fallujah.

**Field Intelligence, Intel:** Intelligence gained in the field, from both human and technical sources, primarily human, and interpreted in the field. U.S. Army snipers, for instance, have a core mission to gather field intelligence, at all times, in combat.

**Fighting knife:** In this book, this term refers to any knife designed and forged for combat.

**1st-505th, 1st BN-505th:** First Battalion of the 505th Parachute Infantry Regiment, 82nd Airborne Division. Since September 11, 2001, deployed in combat in Afghanistan and Iraq. At the time of this writing, on combat deployment in Baghdad, Iraq.

**FLASH, or FLASH FLASH FLASH:** U.S. military radio code, also used by CIA Directorate of Operations, meaning, *I am under fire.* When FLASH is the first word in a written message, it also indicates *Immediate action, now.*

**IED:** Improvised Explosive Device, often dug into sides of roads, or beneath asphalt or dirt in the middle of a road, but also, simply placed in mud and under trash near sidewalks in Iraq and thrown out of taxis. Also known as a roadside bomb. Often placed in carcasses of dead animals. Detonated by remote control, cell phones, and other electronic means, and also, command-detonated.

**In the black, put it in the black:** Shoot a bull's-eye or center mass.

**Iraq, the Iraq War:** Drawn by British mapmakers in London in 1919 from the former Mesopotamia, which was part of the Turkish Ottoman Empire, Iraq in the last quarter of the twentieth century and the first decade of the twenty-first century has become a battleground between three very distinct peoples—the Sunni Arabs, the Shiite Arabs, and the Kurds—forced by the British to be ruled by a central government in Baghdad. Sunni Arabs, heavily supported by British colonial rulers in order to please Sunni Arab sheikhs in neighboring, oil-rich Saudi Arabia, held the reins of power in Iraq from 1920 to 2003.

Roughly 20 percent of Iraq is Sunni Arab, 20 percent Kurdish, and the remaining 60 percent, Shiite Arab. The Baathist dictatorship of Saddam Hussein murdered over 300,000 Kurds and Shiite Arabs between 1978 and 2003, including summary executions of political prisoners at Abu Ghraib prison (see Mike Tucker's *Hell is Over: Voices of the Kurds after Saddam*). One of the most accurate observations of Iraq, since the fall of Saddam, was made by Gunnery Sergeant Harrington of Fox Company, Second Battalion Sixth Marine Regiment, in Fallujah, Western Iraq, on March 22, 2006: "Twenty percent of this country, the Sunnis, fucked over 80 percent of this country: the Shiite and the Kurds. And that 80 percent, the Shiite and the Kurds, are never, never going to let the people who raped their mothers and murdered their fathers back into power, running the show from Baghdad or any other city."

The Iraq War has been referred to by U.S. troops in-country with many names; however, the appellation given it by Marine

Scout/snipers and Marine infantry in Fallujah in the winter of 2005–06 strikes the bull's-eye: "Bush's Goat Fornication." President Bush ordered the invasion of Iraq on March 19, 2003, to end the Baathist dictatorship of Saddam Hussein; Bush's main argument to the United Nations and the world was that Saddam Hussein, in violation of UN resolutions, continued to possess chemical, biological, and nuclear weapons of mass destruction. Baghdad was seized but not secured on April 9, 2003, by elements of the U.S. Army 3rd Infantry Division and 1st Marine Division. The capture, and subsequent hanging, of Saddam Hussein for his war crimes did not end the Iraq War. At the time of this book's publication in December 2008, no weapons of mass destruction have been found in Iraq.

In fall 2007, the only secure, relatively peaceful area of Iraq which welcomes American and Coalition civilians and military personnel is the autonomous region of Iraqi Kurdistan; the rest of Iraq remains at war. Mike Tucker was the first American author to suggest a three-nation-state solution to end the Iraq War, in May 2005, with all U.S. and Coalition troops leaving Iraq; U.S. full support of an independent Kurdistan, within the borders of present Iraqi Kurdistan; and at least one U.S. Army division based in Kurdistan, along with a permanent security agreement between America and Kurdistan (see epilogue of Tucker's *Among Warriors In Iraq*). Since then, the U.S. author and diplomat Peter K. Galbraith and the U.S. author and journalist Thomas Friedman have also backed similar plans, focusing on U.S. support for an independent Kurdistan, as an exit strategy for the war that Bush has failed to execute as a commander in chief and has yet to win: the Iraq War.

**Iraqi Army, IA, IAs:** All terms for Iraqi Army soldiers.

**Iraqi Kurdistan:** Autonomous region of Northern Iraq, defined geographically by the Gara and Zagros mountain ranges, settled by the Kurds for over 6,000 years. The Kurds of Iraq, led by Mala Mustafa Barzani, declared revolution on September 11, 1961, to forge a nation. On October 15, 2005, 98 percent of the Kurds voted in favor of Kurdish independence (see Peter Galbraith's magnificent book, *The End of Iraq*).

**Iraqi Police, IP, IPs:** The Iraqi Police.

**Kentucky windage:** Knowing how to estimate wind and range with nothing but your naked eye and your gut instinct.

**Know for a fact:** U.S. military slang for, *This is true, knowledge gained at firsthand.*

**Know this:** U.S. military slang, which means, *What I am about to tell you is true.*

**Leupold 10x scope:** A very rugged, reliable, and combat-proven scope used by U.S. Marine Scout/snipers, British Army SAS snipers, and other elite snipers; "10x" means "Ten Power," and designates this particular sniper's scope. Used on M24 sniper rifle, SR-25, M14, and other sniper rifles.

**Light Infantry, light infantrymen:** In this book, both terms refer to 10th Mountain division soldiers and commanders. Skilled on all small arms and heavier weapons, such as mortars, rocket launchers, and heavy-caliber machine guns, light infantrymen move hard and fast on foot on any terrain, and can patrol on deep reconnaissance and carry out other Special Operations missions when trained and tasked.

**M4:** U.S. Army assault rifle. Fires 5.56mm (NATO). The M4 has a telescopic buttstock, is lightweight and reliable, and pops up quick on your shoulder. Excellent for urban combat, and for jungle, desert, and mountain combat. Superior to the U.S. Marine infantry M16A-4 in every way but stopping power (both rifles fire a varmint round, 5.56). U.S. Army rifle teams at Fort Benning have fired bull's-eyes with the M4 at 800 meters.

**M4/M203:** The M4/M203 assault rifle/grenade launcher, which fires both 5.56mm ammunition and 40mm grenades. Combat effective range for the M203 grenade launcher is 300 meters. First fielded in the Vietnam War, the M203 grenade launcher is the most versatile small-arms weapon fielded by the U.S. military. Issued to U.S. Army infantry, all U.S. Special Operations, and to U.S. Marine Force Reconnaissance, and Reconnaissance units. Marine infantry carries the M16A-4/M203.

**M14:** 7.62x51mm (NATO) assault rifle. Fires both semiautomatic (single shot) and full automatic; 20-round magazine, with both wooden and plastic stocks. In active service in the U.S. military since 1957, the M14 is still fielded by the U.S. Army and Marines in Iraq and Afghanistan, and by U.S. Special Operations around the world. Combat effective out to 800 meters with a standard-issue barrel, and lethal and accurate out to 1,000 meters with a match-grade barrel. Often carried by U.S. Army snipers, and also by designated marksmen in U.S. Army infantry and U.S. Marine infantry.

**M24:** American sniper rifle, standard issue to all U.S. Army snipers. A 7.62x51mm caliber long-barreled bolt-action sniper rifle, accurate out to 1,000 yards (915 meters). One of the top-drawer sniper rifles in the world, and nearly the same as the Marine Scout/sniper issue rifle, the M40 A3 7.62x51 (NATO) bolt-action sniper rifle.

**M240B 7.62x51mm (NATO) medium machine gun:** The workhorse of U.S. Army infantry, a fairly heavy machine gun for light infantry but with an excellent reputation for not breaking down in combat. Mounted on gun trucks and also carried on foot patrols by U.S. Army infantrymen. Referred to as a *machine gun.*

**Ma Deuce:** Browning M2 .50 caliber heavy machine gun. Essentially the same heavy machine gun that the U.S. Army and Marine Corps have used to good effect in combat since WWII. Mounted on tanks, Humvees, and guard posts.

**Operation Anaconda:** Spearheaded by U.S. and British Special Forces, including Delta Force and SAS, Operation Anaconda targeted Taliban and Al-Qaeda strongholds near the Pakistan border in February–March 2002. Tenth Mountain Division and the 101st

Airborne/Air Assault Division were heavily engaged against fortified mountain positions of the Taliban/Al-Qaeda forces, as were U.S. Army Rangers. Most of the fighting was between 8,000 and 12,000 feet, making resupply for the Coalition forces very difficult, as American combat helicopters are not designed to operate for extended periods of time at those altitudes, in thin air.

**PEQ, AN/PEQ-2A Aiming Light:** Infrared laser device, invisible to the naked eye, mounted on U.S. military rifles, which can also be used as a handheld illuminator/pointer. Powered by AA batteries.

**Rangers:** *See* U.S. Army Rangers.

**Rangers Lead The Way!:** Motto and core philosophy of U.S. Army Rangers, who never hesitate to carry the fight to the enemy. In their philosophy and actions, the Rangers resemble the Spartans of ancient Greece.

**Remote-detonated:** You don't have to see what you are destroying. A cell phone operated five miles away from an IED can be used to remote-detonate the IED.

**Roadside bomb:** *See* IED.

**SAW M249:** Squad Automatic Weapon (SAW) 5.56mm (NATO) light machine gun for U.S. Army infantry and U.S. Marine infantry. Referred to as a light machine gun, it provides 80 percent of the squad's firepower.

**September 11th:** On September 11, 2001, on orders from the terrorist leader of Al-Qaeda, Osama bin Laden, nineteen Al-Qaeda terrorists, fifteen of whom were from Saudi Arabia, hijacked United Airlines and American Airlines passenger jets taking off from Boston, Massachusetts; Newark, New Jersey; and Dulles, Virginia. Bound for the West Coast, each passenger jet was top-loaded with fuel. Carrying box cutters, the Al-Qaeda terrorists penetrated airport security, boarded the first class section in each jet, and once in flight, sliced the throats of pilots and passengers, commandeered the jets, and carried out their suicide attacks on the World Trade Center in New York City, the cultural and financial capital of the United States, and the Pentagon, the U.S. military headquarters, directly south across the Potomac River from Washington, D.C.

Passengers on United 93, hearing on their cell phones that the other hijacked planes had crashed into the World Trade Center and Pentagon, fought back against the Al-Qaeda terrorists on board; in the chaos and struggle, United 93 crashed in a field in Western Pennsylvania. Consensus among historians of September 11th is that United 93 was headed to Washington, to destroy either the White House or the U.S. Capitol Building. As of December 2008 Osama bin Laden remains at large, reportedly in the remote, rugged mountains bordering Afghanistan and Pakistan.

**Sidearm:** In this book, *sidearm* refers to the U.S. Army issue 9mm Beretta semiautomatic pistol, which fires a 15-round magazine. Otherwise, it is a term common to the U.S. and British military, and refers to any semiautomatic or double-automatic pistol of heavy caliber, such as a Colt Commander .45 caliber semiautomatic, an HK USP .45 semiautomatic, or a Glock 21 .45 caliber. Combat veterans of any era will say "sidearm," and also, "piece," when referring to any semiautomatic or double-automatic pistol.

**Special Forces:** *See* U.S. Army Special Forces.

**SR-25:** The SR-25 7.62x51mm (NATO) semiautomatic sniper rifle, favored by U.S. Navy SEALS and U.S. Army Special Operations. Combat effective range is classified.

**Stalking:** The art and craft of tracking your enemy without being detected, on any terrain. Stalking is one of the primary skills of a U.S. Army sniper.

**Task Force 1Panther:** Commanded by Lieutenant Colonel Brian Drinkwine, Task Force 1Panther raided Al-Qaeda and other terrorist and insurgent forces in Fallujah and Western Iraq from early September 2003 to March 27, 2004, when it was relieved by 1st Marine Expeditionary Force.

Delta Force commandos and U.S. Army Special Forces played a key role in Task Force 1Panther's raiding success, contributing significantly to the 80 percent counterterrorist hit rate in Fallujah, unmatched by any Coalition force in Fallujah to this day. Built around 1st-505th, Task Force 1Panther was manned primarily by paratroopers, and also contained the following elements: Attack Company, 1-32, 10th Mountain light infantry; U.S. Army Special Forces; U.S. Army military intelligence; U.S. Army sappers. Special

Operations attachments in December 2003–January 2004 were elements of the SAS, U.S. Navy SEALS, and U.S. Army Rangers.

**10th Mountain Division:** Formed during WWII to raid, assault, seize, and hold mountain redoubts in Europe held by Nazi German and Italian forces, 10th Mountain Division has become, in our time, the most battle-experienced light infantry in the U.S. military. From the Battle of Mogadishu, when 10th Mountain light infantrymen rescued U.S. Army Rangers and Delta Force commandos on October 3, 1993, in the heaviest combat U.S. forces had seen since the Vietnam War, to Afghanistan and Iraq since September 11th, 10th Mountain Division has deployed more often than any other U.S. Army division. Their headquarters is Fort Drum, in upstate New York, about thirty miles south of the Canadian border.

**Types of Firing Positions:**

*Prone Supported:* Lying on your belly, directly behind your weapon, with legs spread shoulder width, and feet flat, toes pointed outward. Weapon can be supported in many ways: bipods, sandbags, rucksacks, window ledge, etc.

*Prone Unsupported:* Just as it sounds: in the prone, without any support. More than likely, you're holding the rifle off the ground.

*Kneeling Unsupported:* One knee down, the other knee at a 90-degree angle, supporting your elbow as you hold the rifle into your shoulder.

*Kneeling Sling Supported:* Same as above; however, the weapon's sling is wrapped around your non-firing bicep, ensuring the arm is pulling the sling tight against your body, giving you a tight hold.

*Standing Supported:* Standing, and leaning forward against a tree, ledge, or any other object that can support the barrel of your rifle, you hold the end of the lower receiver, right underneath the barrel, with your non-firing hand.

*Standing Unsupported:* Standing sideways, with non-firing shoulder in front, and with your hips pushed forward, your front elbow pressed down toward your front hip, supporting the barrel of your rifle.

*Hawkins:* One bipod leg extends out from your non-firing side. You grab the bipod with your non-firing hand, the buttstock of the rifle in your shoulder. Used in the kneeling and standing positions.

**U.S. Army:** Foremost land fighting force of the United States, the U.S. Army was formed in the American Revolutionary War (1775–1781) under General George Washington, who crossed the Hudson in the fall of 1781 with the main body of the Revolutionary Army, led an epic forced march south, and won the war at Yorktown, Virginia.

The U.S. Army was pivotal in defeating the Imperial German Army in WWI and the Nazi German Army, the Japanese Imperial Army, and the Imperial Italian Army in WWII. Since September 11, 2001, the U.S. Army has been heavily engaged in Afghanistan, Iraq, the Horn of Africa, and with its Special Operations Forces, throughout the world. The majority of the Special Operations Forces in United States Special Operations Command (U.S. SOCOM) are U.S. Army forces: U.S. Army Special Forces, Delta Force, and U.S. Army Rangers. The U.S. Army 18th Airborne

Corps, comprised of three legendary divisions—the 10th Mountain Division (light infantry), 101st Airborne/Air Assault Division, and 82nd Airborne Division—can raid from the sky with paratroopers and with very potent airmobile capabilities, by helicopter. General Ulysses S. Grant in the U.S. Civil War, General "Black Jack" Pershing in WWI, and General George S. Patton in WWII are some of the most respected U.S. Army commanders.

**U.S. Army Rangers, Rangers:** Legendary at raids and reconnaissance, the Rangers possess a remarkable battle record that extends back to the French and Indian Wars. Under Brigadier General William O. Darby in WWII, the Rangers led countless raids in North Africa, Italy, and Western Europe, and are famed for their actions at Pointe du Hoc, Normandy, France on D-Day, June 6, 1944. Rangers are also paratroopers and exceptionally well skilled in Special Operations. A core mission for Rangers is to assault and secure hostile airfields. In our time, U.S. Army Rangers often support Delta Force on counterterrorist missions and are highly skilled in all facets of Special Ops. The Rangers consist of three battalions: 1st BN 75th Rangers, based at Hunter Air Field, Savannah, Georgia; 2nd BN 75th Rangers, based at Fort Lewis, Washington; and 3rd BN 75th Rangers, based at Fort Benning, Georgia. The 75th Ranger Regiment, one of the key elements in U.S. Special Operations Command (U.S. SOCOM) is presently engaged in Afghanistan, Iraq, and other terrain.

**U.S. Army Special Forces, Special Forces:** U.S. Army Special Forces were born of the U.S. and Canadian Special Service Brigade in

WWII, which fought with great valor and distinction in Italy. U.S. Army Special Forces are masters of guerrilla warfare and have forgotten more than any other branch of the U.S. military can remember about counterinsurgency. Special Forces are presently engaged against Al-Qaeda, the Taliban, and other terrorists and insurgents in Afghanistan, the Near East, Africa, Europe, and the Far East.

**U.S. Marine Corps:** An elite American fighting force, founded at Tun's Tavern in Philadelphia on November 10, 1775. The Marine slogan, "First to fight," comes from their history of going on point in clandestine actions (U.S. Force Reconnaissance Marines), guerrilla war (U.S. Reconnaissance Marines and U.S. Marine infantry), and conventional war (all U.S. Marine forces). U.S. Marine Raiders in WWII laid the foundation for contemporary U.S. Marine Special Operations. U.S. Marine infantry and reconnaissance units are presently engaged in guerrilla war in Afghanistan and Iraq. Force Recon has also been heavily engaged since September 11, 2001, globally, in counterterrorist actions against Al-Qaeda. Marine infantry (Special Ops capable) has a core mission to assault, engage, and prevail in combat actions, and also carries out the following missions: deep reconnaissance, raids, prisoner of war rescue, search and rescue, and embassy evacuation.

**Vietnam War:** 1961–1975. Also referred to in the Far East as the American Indochinese War, to distinguish it from the French Indochinese War (1946–1954). Won by the North Vietnamese Army and Viet Minh, the Vietnam War was both a guerrilla war and a conventional war, with the NVA and Viet Minh enjoying sanctuaries in Laos and Cambodia. Major Archimedes L. A. Patti, U.S. Army and OSS, wrote prophetic field intelligence analyses while on joint operations with Viet Minh guerrillas in 1945, which underlined the futility of trying to stop Ho Chi Minh from leading a united Vietnam to independence. Major Patti was ignored by the U.S. State Department in the first Truman administration (1945–1948). Over two million Vietnamese died in the Vietnam War, along with over 58,000 Americans.

**Western Iraq:** Known as Western Mesopotamia until the British changed the map in 1919, seizing Mesopotamia from the Turks' Ottoman Empire, and creating the map of Iraq. Western Iraq is strongly Sunni Arab, and the tribes in Western Iraq contributed significantly to the British-favored Sunni elite in Iraq. The Sunni Arabs of Western Iraq, and all Iraq, only numbered 20 percent of the country, but thanks in great part to British and American support, along with military and foreign aid from the Soviet bloc during the Cold War (1945–1989), the Sunnis controlled Iraq from 1920 until April 9, 2003, when Saddam Hussein's Baathist dictatorship was defeated by the U.S.-led Coalition forces. Since April 2003, a fierce guerrilla war has gone down in Western Iraq, which continues at the time of this writing.

**World War II (WWII):** The Second World War. September 1, 1939 to September 2, 1945. Began with Hitler's attack on Poland and his conquest of France and all Western Europe. British and Commonwealth forces were alone in leading global counterattack against both Nazi Germany and Imperial Japan until December 7, 1941, when the Japanese Navy's assault on Pearl Harbor, Hawaii, brought America into the war. Soviet communist forces, most notably in the Soviet victory at Stalingrad, were crucial to the defeat of Nazi Germany. General Dwight D. Eisenhower commanded Allied Forces in North Africa, the Mediterranean, Western Europe, and Northern Europe, and accepted unconditional surrender from Nazi Germany on May 1, 1945. General Douglas MacArthur, commander of all Allied forces in the Pacific, accepted unconditional surrender from the Imperial Japanese in Tokyo Bay on September 2, 1945, ending WWII.

# BIBLIOGRAPHY

Coll, Steve. *Ghost Wars: The Secret History of the CIA, Afghanistan, and bin Laden, from the Soviet Invasion to September 10, 2001.* New York: Penguin, 2004.

Galbraith, Peter. *The End of Iraq: How American Incompetence Created a War without End.* New York: Simon & Schuster, 2006.

Lewis, Bernard. *The Assassins: A Radical Sect in Islam.* New York: Basic Books, 2003.

Shakespeare, William. *Henry V.* London: Penguin, 1994.

Wright, Lawrence. *The Looming Tower: Al-Qaeda and the Road to 9/11.* New York: Alfred A. Knopf, 2007.

# INDEX